Leaping the
Vicarage Wall

Leaping the Vicarage Wall

Leaving Parish Ministry

Ronni Lamont

continuum

Published by the Continuum International Publishing Group

The Tower Building   80 Maiden Lane
11 York Road   Suite 704
London   New York
SE1 7NX   NY 10038

www.continuumbooks.com

First published 2011

British Library Cataloguing-in-Publication Data
A catalogue record for this book is available from the British Library.

ISBN 978-1441-12018-2

Designed and typeset by Fakenham Prepress Solutions, Fakenham, Norfolk NR21 8NN
Printed and bound in India

With thanks to my husband and children, without whom I would be a lesser person.

CONTENTS

ACKNOWLEDGEMENTS

Many thanks go to all the people who contributed to this book. This includes archdeacons, a bishop, several theological colleges and two local training courses. Special thanks go to the very brave people who told me their stories and then approved those accounts that are included in this piece of work. All names have been changed to maintain confidentiality.

LIST OF ABBREVIATIONS

APCM	annual parochial church meeting
CDM	Clergy Disciplinary Measure
CME	continuing ministerial education
MDR	ministerial development review
NSM	non-stipendiary ministers
PCC	parochial church council

INTRODUCTION

This morning I cycled ten miles through what we refer to as the 'Kentryside' to the next town along the A2. There is a cycle route – Number 1, that takes cyclists down through the lanes and creek-sides of Kent that you can't see from the M2. I met perhaps ten cars en route, and a few cyclists. The lovely ride helped me to think about my life, and how much it has changed in 2 years.

Two years ago we were 48 hours from the Big Move. Out of a vicarage, to a town that we knew very little about, and a house that we knew was going to need expenditure for the rest of our lives. Our eldest had graduated the summer we moved, and had just started her new job. At the end of the month she moved out. The youngest finishes university later this month, and will be heading into the rest of his life shortly afterwards.

I was ordained a Deacon in September 1992. I have a sampler on my study wall to remind me, made by my children's godmother, who is also our godchildren's mother. Two years ago I left parish ministry, I leapt the vicarage wall, and set out to discover if I could make a living using the skills and abilities that I had.

> The disconnect between what clergy are expected to do, to achieve ('Be a fresh expression! Keep paying the quota! Both! And!) and the means by which clergy are expected to achieve all this (sustaining the pattern of Herbertism), is getting bigger and bigger. It is impossible. So they leave.[1]

I left parish ministry in September 2008. We had a huge 'All Age' service, followed by brunch, and then the ex-vicarage family drove off to their new home 30 miles away, in the neighbouring diocese (just) and our own home. We'd moved house 2 days prior to my last service.

In between, I was a curate, team vicar and then vicar, working in three very different parishes, all to different effect.

Shortly after my last service, I led a study day on work–life balance for my previous archdeaconry colleagues. One of them was clearly unhappy with the decision that I had made to move out of parish ministry, even angry. Nearly 2 years later we discussed his reaction as part of the research for this book. What impacted upon me more though was the reaction from previous colleagues when I attended the diocesan conference a few months later, by which time it looked as if I could indeed make a living as a freelance. Many of my colleagues were not so much angry or unhappy as plain jealous. 'How did you do it?' was a commonly asked question. How indeed?

The decision of a parish priest to leave parish ministry is profoundly difficult. As a colleague friend said 'but Ronni, where's your vocation?' Where indeed? Too close to 'How indeed?' For them it seemed like a good question, to me it didn't even need to be asked. How could a parish priest feel that working outside of the parish, with 15 years to go before pension day, was living within 'my vocation'? Where was God in all this, to ask the most basic of questions in reference to vocation? And how could I still be a priest but work completely outside of the usual institutional boundaries?

I started contacting people that I knew who had done exactly as I did – left parish ministry and now work in different field. Some, like me, feel a bit like a satellite, orbiting around the established church and dipping in and out through training and writing. Others work in seemingly unrelated fields. But, what I am sure of, is that this is becoming more common than before and that the pressure on parish clergy is going to force more people to look for something they can do as a priest where the personal and family cost is not so high.

This book is an exploration of the factors involved, as well as a glimpse into the lives of people like myself, who've 'leapt the vicarage wall' and found a new and fulfilling ministry in the world outside of the vicarage.

CHAPTER 1
My personal journey

I have always believed in God. As a child, I remember having conversations in my head with God, walking along, standing in the garden, wherever. My family were deeply committed church goers of the traditional Anglican variety, although my father had been Congregational as a child and young man; one of my earliest memories was of him being confirmed into the Church of England. What I remember was that he went out at night, to a group, after he got home from work. As he rarely went out after work, it clearly registered. Apparently my paternal grandmother was the organist at their local church, so he was also raised in a churchgoing environment. My mother was brought up in a small Surrey village, so church going was part of the warp and weft of her life.

We moved to a new town when I was seven, and my parents joined the old church in the middle of the growing town. But my mother realized that there was little at that church for three children, so we were despatched up the road to one of the new estate churches, which had thriving children and young people's work going on. It was far more evangelical, and my elder brother and I stayed there for many years. My younger brother took up bell ringing and so became part of my parents extended church community.

So I went through a very evangelical phase, and that moved into a charismatic phase as the church moved in that direction. By now I was in the youth group, and three of us eventually were ordained from that cohort – not a bad record. One is now a bishop, the other, who was our best man, sadly died a few years ago. We were well led by our (paid) youth leader, so when this thriving group moved on to college and university, we moved into Christian Unions.

During that pre-college time, the youth group ran its own drama group. Drama was very well taught at one of the big local comprehensive schools, and this overflowed into the church. The church there left us to get on with it, and we produced Christian shows, exploring our stories and our faith. The lad who would become my husband was one of the drama movers and shakers. He moved on to college, and I followed a year later, and we continued to work together, with him directing pieces of dance-based theatre for the chapel at college, and then moving into local churches.

The drama enabled us to work on what we believed, to give a safe place for us to work on our faith. The college had a Christian Union, which was the usual 'tending towards evangelical' group, alongside the chapel and chaplain, and a couple of very Anglo catholic young men who started 'the Community of the Holy Name'. This meant that the community had lots of safe space for exploring faith, and because the college had an Anglican foundation, going to chapel was part of my life. Few others attended, but I didn't mind that.

When my husband got his first teaching post we moved to Nottingham, and the drama became a large part of our lives. We carried on producing shows and workshops, travelling and enjoying the company of like-minded people. During this time, we found a church where our drama was encouraged and supported.[1] We both taught in Nottingham comprehensive schools. I taught science, with drama and dance, in a mining school, including the period of the strike of the 1980s, and then worked part time following the birth of our two children.

Following the birth of the second, my job disappeared and I was offered a different school on my return from maternity leave. I didn't want to start again in another school, and was already dissatisfied with part-time teaching. As most of the satisfaction I got from teaching was from my role as head of year and the pastoral interaction that gave, I was wondering if I should look outside of teaching. A job came up facilitating dance in the youth clubs run by the county council, with a focus on urban priority areas. This post was to be part of a growing creative arts team, but I was the first member to be appointed. I spent the next year working mainly at night around the toughest areas of the city and surrounding towns.

It was during this time that I began to wonder what I should really be doing with my life. Giving birth changes your perspective on life, and I was aware of a very high-sounding feeling: that of wanting to make the world a better place for my children to live in. When the local diocese advertised for a Youth Officer, it seemed like the answer to my prayers. And I very nearly got the job too …

So I talked to my vicar about working for the church. As women couldn't be ordained priest at the time (late 1980s) I didn't click quite how vehemently he was opposed to women priests. He supported my application for ordination to the diaconate, and after the usual selection process I found myself accepted to train for stipendiary ministry.

As there is a theological college in Nottingham, I duly applied for a place there and was accepted. There are more comments about my training later in this book, but it was not easy. At this point, my husband had got a job at the BBC in London, and commuted down once or twice a week, staying in friend's spare beds for one or two nights. The children were both preschool, at the local nursery. We found a brilliant child minder to look after them while I was at college, and it was agreed that on the mornings that I needed to drop them before getting to college, I could miss chapel.

After college I found it hard to get my first post. I finally found one in St Albans, which was over and above the diocesan quota, as my salary was paid by the church that employed me. After an interview with the diocesan people, I was ordained in September 1992 and worked at that church for four years. The children were 5 and 6 as I was ordained.

The priesting of women was passed by General Synod 2 months later, and I was part of the first batch of women priests in the diocese. My family made a banner while I was away on retreat. As we all processed round the cathedral following the service, an appreciative 'ah' went up – there it was – 'Hurrah for Mum' in red and green on some spare wallpaper. We were all on the front of the local paper – few women at that time in full-time ministry had school-aged children.

The impact of my work on the family was a real shock to all of us. Sunday had four or five services, depending if it was a baptism Sunday: 8 o'clock, 9.15, 11 and 6.30. Baptisms were at 3 o'clock every other week. For my first year or so, I didn't attend the 8 o'clock, as a (male) priest covered that on their own. But the 9.15 parish communion and matins at 11 had two clergy – one to lead and preside and the other to preach. Evensong was also covered by two clergy. There were three of us most of the time – the vicar, another curate and myself, but if you were on baptisms as well … it was hard work, and I was totally reliant on my husband for childcare during the services.

I also worked five other days. At first I took Saturday off, to be with the family, but once I was on the wedding rota that became less secure. And we had a lot of weddings – I always have had – because the church was a fine traditional building, with a spectacularly good choir and organist. During the week I ran two toddler groups, helped out with the funerals, visited and started groups for the younger women and a reading group for others. Then there were study groups for Advent and Lent, school assemblies, etc. Pressure came from an unexpected area as the church said morning prayer after the school run, but evening prayer daily at 5 p.m. So I would pick up the children, feed them and then we'd kilter down to church, kids supplied with sticker books and crayons to keep them happy while I said the office. As a treat, Friday tea was at McDonald's as a reward for being good during these services.

Christmas was always tough. The church had a crib service at tea time, which I ran, and it grew and grew. I loved taking this service – the faces full of expectation, and the parents relieved at somewhere to take the children to get out and use up some of the waiting time. We had Christmas cake and mince pies afterwards, and many returned every year. But then there was a carol service in the evening, complete with queues to get in, before 'midnight' and the run of Christmas services, which were just like a Sunday pattern. My children were often awake not long after I'd fallen into bed.

Christmas lunch was a great idea of my husband's; we went to Marks and Spencer, and – oh the luxury – everyone chose what they wanted to eat on Christmas day from the ready-food section. They were often odd selections of food, but everyone was happy. We finished with the Christmas pudding and cake prepared long before, and then I would fall asleep. And then I usually covered the Sunday after Christmas day too, before having a Sunday off the weekend after that.

The last year at this church was without a vicar. He had retired. Christmas Day was on a Monday – the worst day for clergy, as you have to 'do' Sunday which then runs into the

Christmas Eve pattern, on into more services for Christmas Day. At the time, Robert Runcie was living in the area, as retired Archbishop of Canterbury. He offered to take the 8 o'clock on Christmas Eve for me – it was the anniversary of his ordination. I didn't tell the folks who was presiding at their service that Christmas Eve, just said that they would be very happy. They were. It was an incredibly kind offer to help two curates, who were struggling to cope with the weight of work they faced that Christmas.

The new vicar arrived and I duly left for my first incumbency, in a new town not far away. If I saw the post today, I would avoid it like the plague, but I was young(er) and inexperienced in the ways of the Church of England. The post was to manage the amalgamation of two district churches, demolishing one and building a new vicarage and 'pastoral centre' on the site. I was told the two congregations had agreed, and I would have a reader and a non-stipendiary minister to assist.

Later I discovered the unhappy story of the larger church, which had lost a vicar when he was accused of having an affair. I also discovered that the smaller church wasn't happy about their building being demolished and neither congregation liked the other lot that much really. Congregations can be very tribal and this was the only church in the area, while the larger church was just yards from the local Methodist church.

It was not a happy time for us. The work load was enormous. Yes, the reader helped with preaching and funerals, but there was an enormous amount for me to do. The plans for change fell apart, and I ended up working with many committees trying to find a way forward for these churches. I was given a curate and then trained another reader, who were both an enormous help. A big factor was being part of a team ministry which was at great discomfort within itself at the time. We also lived in a house that was not built as a vicarage and far smaller than it should have been. My husband and I used what was supposed to be the study as a bedroom, as we only had two decent-sized rooms upstairs – the others were very small indeed. People still expected meetings at the vicarage, but we quickly began using other places. My husband was driving to work daily, as the trains were not so good, and the children were growing up, becoming teenagers in a town where they found themselves in a strange place socially.

We were all very stressed by the time I found my next incumbency. St Somewhere was one church, not two, with a smaller population to care for. We needed to find somewhere where the children could flourish and be happy, and they were. The vicarage was an amazing house, far bigger than we'd had before (or since!), and they both ended up at a local school where they found friends who were people like them. The commute to work was eased, we sold a car, and life looked better.

But the pressure of the work remained. The house was big enough for meetings, and the church was just across the lawn, so that helped, but the regular stream of people at the door didn't. I discovered that the previous incumbent's wife was ordained and did a lot of pastoral work in the parish. The most active reader died 6 months after I arrived, leaving me with one reader who worked full time and had a young family. The workload arrived at the vicarage, and I had to deal with it.

I was good as a vicar. The contact with the local (church) school grew stronger and stronger. I loved the work there and the parish was pleased with the relationship. More and more young families came to our monthly 'family' service, but fewer of the older congregation came along. So we decided to change the service pattern, so that the 'fifth' Sunday matins became a monthly service after the family service. Numbers rose again. The wedding numbers grew, as did the numbers of people requesting baptism. Funeral numbers remain constant, but the overall workload increased.

I was just finishing my MA, which I started previously. I completed my dissertation research in the local school and wrote up the paper.[2] This was picked up by a publisher, who wanted me to work it up into a book. By now, I had a full-time curate, who was working alongside me. So, a year after she arrived, I took time out to write the book, and she ran the church for 3 months.

It was a deeply significant time for both of us. Our youngest began university as I began my study leave. We had a holiday on our own at the beginning, and a few days away at the end. In between we visited people over weekends. I remembered what the word 'weekend' means to most people. I hardly went to church at all. I sent in my manuscript, and waited for the book to be published.

By now, it was clear that if I was to live to draw my pension, I needed to work outside of parish ministry. We began to look at the possibility of my going freelance and working in training and writing – something my husband had done as we moved to St Somewhere, and was enjoying real success. I had done some training in Godly play before the research, and was interested in spreading the gospel of Godly play wherever I could. The diocesan children's officer was already a colleague, and I worked with her from time to time. I had also trained in spiritual direction – a special form of listening and reflecting with folk about the faith journey. We still had our house in Nottingham, which had been let throughout my ministry. So we thought about the possibility of moving back to the Midlands, which we had both loved, but realized that it was too far from the centre of my husband's work. I had also trained as a 'Section 48' school inspector (inspecting church schools after Ofsted), and was inspecting for Canterbury diocese – where I also had contacts.

At this point, Rochester made their children's officer redundant, and I began to get calls asking me to cover some of her training work. I had writing commissions, mainly designing services and acts of worship for a church resource magazine. I was being asked to talk at conferences, to lead drama workshops, to do all sorts of things, but I couldn't, because I couldn't carve the time out from the parish. It began to look as if I could actually make a living without parish ministry. I was then approached by my publishers, and asked to take over part of their assembly web resource.[3] Once I was also doing this, there was a basic income that was guaranteed.

We sold the house, and began looking for somewhere we could afford within an hour's commute from London. The rest, as they say, is history. While I was going through the year or so prior to resignation, I was well supported by a somewhat disappointed archdeacon, who tried his hardest to get the diocese to find something part-time so that I could feel my talents were being used. The suffragan bishop was also very helpful. He really wanted me to take a part-time parish, but as much of my work is at weekends, that wouldn't have solved the problem. He helped me to see the move within the context of my vocation, and as he's an imaginative bishop, could see that maybe this was indeed the next step for me. I couldn't tell anyone in the parish, as I wasn't sure when I would be moving on, but I do have to give credit to the brave woman who I had recruited as new church-warden, only to turn around and tell her that she was going to be steering the parish through a vacancy in her first year in the post. Most people would have backed out, but she didn't.

Why did I leave? At the time, I felt it was to release my skills and talents, to be able to work for the whole Church, not just that bit of it. And I still think so. But, with time, I can see that my feelings about what I do now mirror those of Felix (see chapter 7). Maybe the expression is that I wanted my life back – I was slowly being squeezed into a vicar-shaped mould, fed up with asserting my right to be the person that I am, not the one that people saw when their eyes saw the collar. I wanted time with my family, my friends, not to have to leave Saturday events so that I could be okay the next morning. And I wanted my privacy back. I wanted to be able to walk around Sainsbury's without people stopping me to talk and look at what I was buying. To be able to buy underwear in the local shops without feeling self-conscious, to be able to walk home without being haled by the local children, nice as it was that they all knew me. I wanted to go on holiday and not worry about who would the undertakers be caring for when I returned. I wanted to tell people to stop being rude to me just because they seemed to think they could and I had no right of reply. I realize now that living in a vicarage was slowly suffocating me.

And my husband wanted his wife back. Not to be second when we were at social events. Not to be ignored when we met parishioners if we were out. And for me to have time, to 'live the dream' as we call it – to be free to really take charge of my diary, to take holidays at short notice and to be there for my children when they need me. When I was on study leave, I was amazed at how I 'slept for England'. I had no idea how deeply tired I was. I did it again after we moved, and I now look younger, my shoulders have lost their tension and I am far fitter.

More importantly, I have been working, without any real break in demand, since I left the parish within my areas of expertise. I have earned enough money to live, not a lot more, but enough. And I know that I am serving the Church as I feel called to do. I still take 'rent a vic' services for people on study leave or on holiday (not the same thing!) and I help out with funerals when I can, so my public ministry still goes on. But the pleasure from teaching and training people, especially in the field of children's spirituality, feels like the real 'me' in action. Leaping the vicarage wall was very, very hard. But it was worth it.

CHAPTER 2
Parish life explored

The local church

'Receive this cure of souls, which is both yours and mine ...'. So says the bishop as a new vicar/rector arrives at their new parish. Already we're into archaic language, and as a good Anglican I'll try and translate jargon as I use it.

The prime task of the parish priest is to lead worship, both on Sundays and at other appropriate times. So most clergy say morning prayer, often in church, daily as well as the Sunday routine. Then there's writing the sermons, choosing the hymns (in collaboration with the church's music people) and leading study groups. Often this extends to training others who lead study groups, to extend and develop the spiritual lives of the congregation. Clergy need to regularly engage with the Bible, as we have to know it well, and what it might be saying for life today. Preparing for a Sunday may take many hours, especially if Sunday includes a 'Family' or 'All Age' service – supposed to be inclusive of everyone, and especially friendly for folks who might be at the beginning of commitment to the church. These services are notoriously difficult to prepare and lead, and some clergy hand the whole thing over to others in their church who may be better at this more informal style of worship.

Leading worship is taken for granted by observers – but some clergy are far more user friendly than others. What isn't widely recognized is how tiring it can be, and how many different skills are needed to do it well.

Most sermons require a lot of work, as they are basically an essay to be spoken aloud. Some are better than others at this, and all preachers find some texts easier to work on than others. Many denominations expect would-be ministers to preach as part of their interview process, but I've never heard of that in the C of E. But a poor preacher is not good for church attendance, and the pews get hard for many of us more quickly if we're bored. And some bishops are awful preachers too – but you only get to hear them from time to time!

The parish priest has within his/her responsibility everyone who lives within the geographic boundary of their parish. That parish is enshrined in Church law (canon law), and is, like a voting ward, marked out clearly, to the vicar at least.

Many of the clergy's problems crop up when people either don't know about or refuse to work within the boundaries that the Church has imposed on the local area. Issues such as 'where can I have my baby baptized?' can get caught up between two neighbouring ministers with differing attitudes to baptizing babies. The church where I was curate baptized anyone's baby who asked. The neighbouring parish didn't, so we 'did' all their babies, causing potential strife between the neighbouring churches, but, and this is important, potential gain or loss of income through the collection at such a service. I also once got caught in the middle of the classic double bind: we were approached by a family who wanted their two children baptized. Their parish priest wouldn't baptize the children, as the parents themselves weren't baptized. When the parents said they would like to be baptized, the priest refused them saying it was just so they could get the children 'done'. This, apparently, was also diocesan policy. We baptized, and later confirmed, the mother and the two girls. The elder of the girls also joined the communion-prior-to-confirmation group, and all are now regular worshippers.

In my last incumbency (where I was vicar), I had a very traditional-looking church, with all the right attributes for many couples seeking a 'venue' for their wedding. We cleaned up on the local wedding scene, and this helped to pay to keep the church standing, as well as towards the very expensive repairs to the organ …. But 25 weddings a year brings a vast amount of work, which as vicar, I had to do. This then, from about a year later, brought in the baptisms of the subsequent babies of those couples (a fabulous re-meeting) who now mainly lived outside of the parish, where it was/still is excruciatingly expensive to buy a house. Alongside that is the request to take a families' funeral of elderly members of the wedding congregation because 'We know you, and you know us' and you see how the joy that we call 'occasional offices' which is the mainstay of Anglican parish life (and income) can become a difficult area of negotiation with other clergy for their permission to carry out rites of passage for folk from their 'cure of souls', which, strictly speaking, should fall to them. The occasional offices become non-occasional, even frequent, and this is increasing as parishes are melded and merged and the numbers of souls increases with every job move. Grace Davie sums up the situation well:

> On the one hand, parishioners have access to their parish church; a right claimed for first marriages and for funerals in particular. The clergy are obliged (and trained) to respond appropriately. One the other hand, such responses take up a considerable amount of time and are, undoubtedly, demanding and costly aspects of ministry. They provide, however, innumerable points of access to an otherwise disinterested population.[1]

So, through the occasional offices, the church reaches much of the population within a parish, but most of those people only come to church when they want something from it – as is their right. But as the Church is now largely in decline, clergy are desperately trying to increase the size of their regular congregation, quite apart from believing that worship is for everyone – and we'd like you all to become Christians in the process. The mix of serving the area with the basic need to spread the gospel can become difficult to juggle, even though we know that serving the area's need is indeed a way of spreading the gospel.[2]

Thus you may not be able to do a whole lot of other work in the parish, and so you come to the crux of most clergy's lives – priorities, pressure and guilt. (Interestingly, and probably very significantly, the one diocese in the country where many churches are growing rather than decreasing is London, where there are far fewer occasional offices.) For churches unlike St Somewhere, which don't catch the 'rites of passage' demands, there may be other demands, such as mega-successful youth work, or even having to sort out regular occurrences of vandalism and theft, along with all the paperwork and feelings of failure to connect that this brings.

> The problem fundamentally comes down to two aspects of the clergyman's [sic] work: first, what the work represents; and second, how the work is expressed.[3]

What a parish priest does, day by day, is a mystery to those outside of the vicarage. It also varies from priest to another, depending on their strengths and interests. How they organize and prioritize is up to each individual minister. The phone rings, someone wants something – how do they decide whether this is urgent and essential, or just a call that needs to be taken,

Edith on the end of the phone pacified and calming down, or is World War Three is really breaking out over someone moving a hassock?

Believe me, I've been there. In the church where I was curate, we had the most beautiful set of hand-made hassocks. Every single one was different, each lovingly made by a good lady (that's an assumption, but I think probably accurate) and many were 'In memory of ...' or 'To celebrate ...'. The church had been re-modelled, very successfully, into two parts: the old high altar (sanctuary) end had been stripped out and carefully carpeted, chairs installed and turned into what we called 'the Lady Chapel'. It seated about 50 people – great for Sunday 8 o'clock/midweek services, smaller weddings and more intimate funerals. It was separated from the main body of the church by the old rood screen, a carved set of uprights from a base at waist height. (We still had the screen at St Somewhere – it was made of iron bars mainly and I referred to it as the 'gorilla cage': as the resident gorilla, I felt I could.) But this church had a different style of hassocks from the Lady Chapel, and one particular lady, let's call her Edith, had taken it upon herself to allocate every hassock a particular place in the body of the church or the Lady chapel. And she knew where every single one should be hanging, for the relief of knees. So when I let the local primary school children pick one that they felt was special and then bring it out to the central space and sit upon it, Edith got quite upset if I (or the children) put them back in the 'wrong' place.

Now, war over the hassocks sounds surreal, but every church has its own version of people trying to hang onto something very important to them about this particular building, and their relationship with it.

Sometimes difficult people have no other outlet but their

faith community. Their involvement in church is loaded with particular significance for them.[4]

For many older people, it's to do with the change that their lives are awash with, and trying to keep the church as a calm centre. There's the old light bulb joke:

How many Anglicans (insert your own denomination) does it take to change a light bulb?—Change?

The other factor is that many people are lonely, especially older people, so calling the vicar for a chat becomes a real option for people contact. And most churches have lots of older people.

The life of a vicar is interrupted frequently by good people, who like Edith, have something that they need to tell you – now and immediately – and that the vicar must listen to and process. Some days it's fine, you have the time and you can handle the conversation. On others, it can feel like the last straw. Yvonne Warren, in her book *The Cracked Pot*, observes:

Clergy are like mice on a wheel – going round and round in circles. They are always trying to be God's represent-ative, especially to the needy and yet, from time to time, feeling within themselves a deep sense of not being good enough or ever achieving enough.[5]

And the question of the vicar's workload is acknowledged as a source of stress:

There is often a lack of information about what church members expect of the minister. What is the measure of ministry being done well?[6]

How does a vicar know they are doing the job well, other than increasing pew coverage at the main service? For many, Sunday attendance is decreasing – often not because people don't want to be there, but because other activities, such as children's Sunday sports, take a higher priority. Trying to start services that are during the week to cater for such people has only recently become more common[7] – the outbreak of the phenomenon called 'Messy Church®',[8] a family-based activity focussed service, which meets during the week or on a Sunday afternoon, illustrates that many people do want meaningful contact with the Church, but Sundays (especially mornings) are just too busy.

> Teaching and pastoring remain. But now there is a distinctive third strand ... now the challenge and calling is first to find people to search for his [God's] children' [sic] and then teach and pastor them.[9]

> An anxious church is beset by initiatives. Mission committees have them; clergy have them; bishops have them; the national church has them ... Wise church people have learned to spot initiatives gathering in the distance, like storm clouds.[10]

Over the last few years, as congregations have dwindled and finances become ever tighter, there have been many initiatives at both national and diocesan level to help parishes engage with the people that they never see within church as well as those who come when they need to. While these often involve excellent training and guidance, somehow for many clergy it feels like another source of guilt; that I'm not doing it right, or somehow, I should be more successful. This is not what the initiatives were designed to do, but it reflects the low self-esteem that is found among many clergy, which is induced through not having clear job descriptions, work–life boundaries and good time management skills.

Every parish has different expectations, and yet these are rarely listed in the 'person profile' – the document that a parish prepares for would-be incumbents to look at. So, for example, when I moved from my first incumbency to my second, I looked for a parish that would welcome my involvement in the local schools. Although in theory, my first parish wanted my involvement with the local schools, by the time I'd been into five primary schools, a special school and a large comprehensive, a huge amount of time was gone from a working week, even with the visits well spread out through a term. So while the parish could see on paper that this was an excellent use of my time, they didn't like the reality that it meant for them as individuals, less time for the vicar to call and talk, listening to their needs and wants, as most congregations want their vicar to do. I looked for parish with a desire for a vicar with a sense of humour: I was once told I was 'flippant' by someone who was clearly looking for a different personality in his vicar. The final description I looked for was someone who is good with that classic 'young families'. That's my area of expertise, but when lots of young families did arrive in church, there were inevitably people who found the change in ambience and focus difficult, but many families enjoyed the contact and are now committed members of that congregation. It is now recognized that, on the whole, younger people like to worship in a different way from those who have been in the church for a while. This means many churches have two completely separate services, to cater for these different needs.

A good work–life balance is rare in Parish clergy, because there is no defining task to be done:

The clergy are in a bad way because of problems. As it was put to me so vividly on a chapter retreat, 'Even if I clear all the paperwork from my desk, there are still 5,000 people out there who need visiting.'[11]

By the time I was into my last incumbency, my family and I had put a lot of carefully constructed boundaries into place. Many of these boundaries are reflected in a later interview with the minister who managed to 'thrive' in his previous post, so I won't repeat them here (see chapter 4). But such practices came from a very tough time in my first incumbency, where I had a huge and very demanding population within my part of a large team parish. (A team parish is where lots of smaller areas have been 'teamed' up, with the aim that clergy support and help each other. This is often done in an area of rapidly expanding populations, such as a New Town – as I was in. As the town grew, the original parishes became unmanageable, so teams were set up, with districts within each team parish. As a team vicar, I had two districts and 14,000 people, within a parish of 66,000.)

In this team parish, one of my two churches would let me know that I'd done something to cause offence by some of the congregation refusing to speak to me, even in church on Sunday. I have to confess to still finding this vaguely amusing, and a fine example of how to shoot yourself in the foot on their part. But being ignored by part of the congregation does hurt, and as their priest, makes the task fairly hard to undertake.

One of the most difficult moments of the clerical year is not a high day such as Easter or Christmas, but that dreaded event, the annual parochial church meeting (APCM). Many churches still call it their annual general meeting. It's a chance to go through the accounts and review the task of the church in that place. Clergy aren't often trained in chairing meetings, so I would take my guide book to the rules and regulations in with me, just to make sure we were acting correctly. That didn't stop one person telling me that 'this is how we do it, the book is clearly wrong'. It was after one such meeting that I contacted the teaching council and seriously thought about going back into school. As I had been a secondary teacher, you can surmise how difficult the APCM had been! I did wonder if I could charge for having my increasingly grey hair dyed on the expenses, but thought that might be objected to.

While the APCM is an annual event, the parochial church council (PCC) has to take place at least five times a year, running the 'business' that an Anglican church can feel like at times. Keeping an eye on budgets and cash flow, organs and a listed building is not why I became a priest, but it is a large part of the minister's role. You do learn very quickly! I always explained to each parish that I was very good at spending money, not so good at budgeting, and they always assumed this was my little joke. By the end, I was good at both, but it is not something that I started ministry seeing as a high priority.

The PCC is an elected group, and most ministers manage to collect largely the PCC that they want after a few years. It's inevitable, but folk who spend each meeting arguing with the chair gradually resign. While this may make meetings flow more easily, it can be a source of criticism from the 'outside' group. Paul Bayes comments:

> Most churches find it very hard to give people space to reflect together on the reasons why decisions are made, and on exactly why their leaders make the choices they do.[12]

People within a church assume that everyone is there for the same reason – the reason that they are there. That is patently not so, but this growing awareness of what a church provides for different people can be a difficult realization for those who have been worshipping and attending with like minded people for years.

One of my initial aims in my last parish was to slowly reduce the average age of people on the PCC, to reflect the younger profile of the church. One very elderly lady who'd been on the PCC for what seemed like most of the entire time the church had been there, thought I was going to take out a 'contract on her' and 'send the boys round'. A kind soul explained to her how lowering the average age worked in reality, and she was still on the Council when she died. The average age fell that year.

A wise friend commented to me that for a minister to stay sane in parish life, they needed a very secure self-image and to be confident in their calling to be both prophet and priest: priest to share the sacraments with the people and prophet to point out where they felt God is leading this place. The advantage of clergy arriving from outside a parish is that they often see all too clearly where the congregation may have got 'stuck' on the journey of faith together. Breaking this news to the congregation can ruffle feathers and cause conflict, but it is part of the role of the minister to be the one who comments from time to time on normative behaviour that needs reflecting upon.

Ecumenical matters

The Church of England usually works with other denominations in the same area, often through Churches Together[13] organizations. This means that the ministers meet regularly for support and dissemination of information, as well as trying to work together whenever possible. There is usually also a ministers/lay people planning committee to organize events. So, in my last parish, we held a shared 'Stations of the Cross' service on Good Friday, and took it in turns to lead, so producing variation on the theme. We also met on Easter Sunday morning for a 'Sonrise' service, and had other events through the year, some social, some overtly spiritual. These groups can be excellent, as ministers share their lives together, and draw the various churches closer.

The wider church

Most parishes have one ordained minister, heading up teams of volunteers who may or may not have been trained for their ministry. Clergy meet together from time to time in local groups called chapters, reflecting the administrative unit called the deanery. There are a number of deaneries in an archdeaconry, and generally two or three archdeaconries per diocese. The area or rural dean, who is also usually in charge of a parish, reports to the archdeacon, who in turn reports to the bishop. But there is very little real power in any of these roles – when there's a problem, the archdeacon will usually be the person who gets involved, reporting to the bishop. One archdeacon described her role as 'the carthorse, while the bishops are the race horses'.

So while there is a clear management structure, in reality parish clergy work on their own most of the time. Chapters are notoriously competitive, and clergy choose their friends carefully. As a woman, I found that the local ordained women would meet informally, and I was often asked by new clergywomen arriving in the deanery to be her informal mentor. As someone who had been around for longer I could advise in administrative or canon law areas. This is a role that I still enjoy, but it is time consuming and sometimes demanding. I found myself increasingly advising on boundaries and work–life issues, as people became established in their working patterns. Although clergy training covers this area, it is only when they find themselves in a parish, dealing with conflicting demands on their time and attention, that ministers realize they need a refresher in the field. As bishops and archdeacons seem often to be workaholics, they are not always modelling a good example to their clergy.

Having arrived at this point, I would like to emphasize the positive side of the job. From outside the vicarage, it is not always possible to see the real pleasure and feeling of a job done well that being a vicar can bring. Although I could now take a wedding without a service book, so well do I know the words, conducting a wedding is rarely a chore. I did enjoy the 'glad rags' element, as did many of the choristers. Seeing people dressed up, having a good day out, and celebrating the love of two people is wonderful. And, as the officiant, I can see what's going on in the church! Everyone else just looks at the happy couple. I loved the wedding where the groom and best man both wore tartan 'Doc Martin' boots: as a Scot, the groom had been encouraged to wear a kilt – so tartan boots were worn instead. But few could see them, apart from me. And grooms in kilts are rarely taught how to sit. And imagine the colour I turned when the groom sat down, legs akimbo, directly opposite me! (Blue Y fronts, if you want to know.) Twice in weddings on consecutive weeks a bride lost her garter on the way up the aisle and I had to snatch it from her ankle during the first hymn ... there's far more to keeping a wedding going than there looks from where the congregation are.

Likewise baptisms: families celebrating the birth of a baby seems like a great idea to me. And asking God to be part of that celebration – yes! Both these services can involve elements of 'crowd control', but so does any event like this. But many churches have an internal tension over baptisms – frequent visitors who they often don't see again until the next child needs baptism – rarely does a church reflect on what is it we do that means these families don't want to come in between?

But the service that can give enormous satisfaction, if that's the appropriate word, is a well-conducted funeral. A chance to assure grieving people that God knows and loves their lost one is a real opportunity. To pitch it so that the family can be comforted in some way, and leave the service recognizing that something significant has just taken place, can make all the stress and pressure worthwhile.

A gathering of clergy will often swap 'funeral stories'. The following happened at my local crematorium, and was during a service a colleague was conducting. Gran had died, and the family requested Judy Garland singing *Somewhere Over The Rainbow* in the middle of the service. The point arrived, the chap in the box at the back put on the CD. Then his mobile phone trilled and he took the call. The song ran into the next track, which was *Ding Dong, The Wicked Witch Is Dead*. My colleague continued the service as if nothing untoward was going on until the chap at the back realized what had happened. I have asked for Judy Garland for my own funeral: when my kids laugh, people may wonder what the joke is!

Weekly services for the faithful, visiting folk in hospital, giving communion to the sick and/or dying: all these are part of the common clergy round. We are often the cement of the local community, known by the local school children from taking their assembly/collective worship, the toddlers from the group that we visit from time to time and people in the locale, who rely on clergy to be there for them at their point of need. Wearing a dog collar in the area makes you different, but sometimes there is a real need to blend back into the background and be treated as a normal person once again.

It is a good life. It can be a wonderful life. But it grows larger, and people grow increasingly more demanding as they expect the church to respond to their needs as consumers. It can be tough. As another wise colleague commented:

> It's not the major dramas that get to you – the adrenaline takes you through the high dramas. It's the grinding nitty gritty that can break you.

CHAPTER 3
Personality and ministry

When I was a small child, I loved the TV programme *All Gas and Gaiters*. This comedy gently ribbed typical churchmen, watching their lives. It starred Derek Nimmo, who gently bumbled his way through life. Other programmes, such as *Father Ted*, have played to the idea of what clergy could be like, perhaps with the real change coming in *The Vicar of Dibley*, where the female cleric did a masterful job in the village, albeit by strange methods from time to time. Revd Geraldine was presented as a real person, rather than the comic book cut-outs in *Father Ted*. We now have *Rev*[1] and great debates in the *Church Times* as to how close this is to a true portrayal. In the meanwhile, we have had several reality TV vicars, whom we have watched through the vagaries and anguish of parish life.

The critical element that underrides such programmes is that the elements of such people's lives that we watch is dependent on the director/producer, who need interesting TV if the ratings are to be maintained, so it's still vicarage life, but not quite as we know it. But these programmes have subtly reinforced the general population to what clergy 'should be like', and many still have quite strange ideas. 'What the vicar is like' is still a topic of conversation at the school gates, and the 'vicar with an earring' (especially if it's a man) still raises eyebrows. Ordained in 1992, I was known, I discovered, as the 'vicar in shorts' for a while, when that was the fashion. The slightest eccentricity can be noted and discussed.

'What a member of the clergy is like' is still up for debate. Many of us like to think we are outside the norm, but alas, alack, many are still quite near to dear Derek Nimmo! However, hope is at hand. Personality indicators and tools for analysis are available, and increasingly used. Thus, we clergy can find out if we really are 'a bit different'.

Over the years since the last world war, more and more psychological tools have become available to the public. These tools give an insight into how each individual functions, and how we all vary. Self-knowledge can be increased along with self-understanding, and these tools are increasingly used by professionals to examine who they are and how they interact with other people.

Myers–Briggs

The Myers–Briggs Type Indicator test was first used in the 1960s and is now gaining in popularity to the extent where people may ask 'What's your Myers–Briggs?' Clergy are certainly expected to know the answer to that question. The types are divided up along four continua, so that I could reply, for example, 'ENFJ' and that makes sense to those who have also undertaken the test.

This system, which classifies people into one of 16 types, was devised following basic Jungian typology and his under-standing of how they flourish. Myers and Briggs took the four Jungian aspects of personality and combined them, giving the 16 different types. Two of the aspects are processes, one aspect is to do with attitude and one with orientation.

The process options relate to situations and how we handle them. They are Sensing versus iNtuition and Thinking versus Feeling. The attitude measure is Judgement versus Perception, and the orientation is Extroversion versus Introversion. The combinations are listed by the capital letters – for example, ENFJ, ISTF – and there are, hence, 16 of these types. The letters indicate the person's preferred way of acting, but do not mean that they never use their shadow side. So while I am usually an extrovert, from time to time (and this is increasing as my type shifts) I enjoy time on my own, working and thinking things through. But after a day in front of my square screen I am glad to meet someone for a chat and social interaction.

Each type will show a different personality and way of carrying out their lives and work. What it is critical for us to note is that this system can help us to see why that person drives me round the bend, while another person is easy to be with, and I can then work to understand why that person is acting in the way that s/he is, and that I am probably equally annoying and difficult (or easy to be with) for them. Myers–Briggs helps us to underline everyone really is unique, and not likely to think or act as I do – and neither of those ways will necessarily be The Right Way. There is a real need for live and let live. The table summarizes the differences between the types.

Preferred Perception process (how I gather and process information) S or N	
Sensing	*iNtuition*
Facts, multi sensory	Abstract, symbol
Real, proven, known	Inspiration, hunch, possibilities
'Eyes tell mind'	'Mind tell eyes'
Preferred Judging process (how I make decisions) T or F	
Thinking	*Feeling*
Logical analysis	Personal consequences
Issues rather than feelings	Principles may be overlooked
Justice, what's fair	Emphasis on sympathy
Other's feelings may get hurt	

Preferred Orientation (how I interact with the world) E or I	
Extrovert	*Introvert*
Outer world, public, social	Inner world, privacy
Groups are energizing	Solitude is refreshing
Speak before I think	Think before I speak
Preferred Attitude (how I undertake tasks) J or P	
Judgement	*Perception*
Ordered, planned	Open, flexible
Like closure, lists welcomed	Further information, other possibilities
Favours coming to clear decisions	Final decisions postponed

Churches often have a Myers–Briggs workshop for their new PCC. Bear in mind that a person's indicator is not fixed – I recently swung from an F to a T, much to my amazement. You can work on your shadow side to try and bring it into play more often, and if you are working with a similar type person, it's sometimes fun to stop and think how someone who has a very different way of interacting with your world would react to what you are planning!

It's also important to recognize that with different personality types comes preferred ways of worship. Different prayer styles, different types of preferred music: there really isn't the 'right' way to pray I'm afraid, just the right way for you. So variety really is the spice of life here. And remember, you aren't 'stuck' with this type for life; if there's something you don't like about your personality, get on with changing it by consciously using your shadow more often. There is no 'better' type either – just how people are. You will prefer certain types, as they affirm you as a person and how you set about doing things, but life would be boring if we didn't have heated discussions, wouldn't it? The trick is to aim towards a balance; so while adults will always fall into these groups, if their score is near the boundary, they are more balanced individuals.

Needless to say, we all use the 'shadow' of our predominant type from time to time, as we need. Some types are more common than others, which helps us to understand when we meet people who feel unusual to us; they belong to a more unusual group. Whether they perceive that as something to be celebrated depends on how high their self-esteem is.

Knowing the Myers–Briggs types of colleagues, and those with whom clergy work, can be very helpful: a bit of knowledge really can go a long way here. It will help to understand that certain people are always going to get impatient with me, as they work in such a different way – and likewise I could get frustrated by their approach to the world. However:

> Francis and Jones (1996) ... found that the main body of Anglican male clergy was introvert. Such people find social gatherings difficult, public occasions embarrassing and would prefer to hide away.[2]

When I was in my first incumbency, the team that I worked within had an away day to explore our Myers–Briggs personality indicators. This was in the year 1997 or so, and was the first time I had really engaged with this tool. There were six of us in the team, and we all came out with different personalities (no surprise there) but the majority were introvert. We had already moved our weekly team meeting from Monday to Tuesday mornings, as one of the team found the meeting too tough after a Sunday, where she was working in her 'shadow side' all day. As highly introverted individual, the services were a sapping experience. As an extrovert, I am often energized by the worship and the two-way movement of energy during the worship.

At St Somewhere, one of my neighbouring clergy colleagues was an introverted North American. That was oxymoronic in itself for many. He is an enormously able man, but shy. And people expect clergy to be 'people people'. Interestingly, many are not. Being able to chat, small talk, is high on the list of requirements in popular clergy. The question of extroversion/introversion is well addressed in *The Human Face of Church* by Sara Savage and Eolene Boyd-Macmillan:

> Some people feel the need to be liked more than others. This difference is in part connected to the extrovert and introvert distinction in human personality. Extroverts feel the need to belong to a group more strongly than introverts; the difference is not about liking people, but on how their brain is wired to maintain an optimum level of stimulus ... extroverts are slightly bored: they are looking for action and this includes seeking out other people. So, the external, social world is fascinating and vital for extroverts. Dorothy Rowe[3] asserts that for extroverts belonging to a group is so important that rejection by the group can threaten the extrovert's vital sense of *being a self*. Thus an extrovert may conform more readily than an introvert in order to be liked .... In contrast ... the introvert functions in such a way that they tend to become over stimulated. Introverts reach overload more quickly. An introvert needs more solitude ... an introvert may not be so devastated by rejection from the group, as the introvert's sense of self comes from personal achievement and the requisite personal clarity. Instead ... introverts may dread invasion *by* the group. An introvert will conform outwardly (while resisting inwardly), simply to be left in peace![4]

An extrovert person is gaining their sense of self by how others react to them. This can be seen in what appears to be a 'need to be needed' that is evident in many clergy, despite their introversion. A tendency to do everything asked of them, to never say 'no', to allow people to walk over them and their personal needs is common among the clergy, and if you sometimes treat others how they are treating you, there can be a quite shocking response. My training incumbent had a very secure sense of self and could be very blunt (he did come from Yorkshire). But people would be surprised at that sometimes, as clergy are still expected to be 'nice', as are the people who worship in their churches:

> The group spirit, or 'ego' of a church, conspires to make conflict a gruelling experience. One contributing factor is the prevailing norm of niceness. People are supposed to be 'nice' in church. Translation: no anger, no disagreement, no problems, *no* conflict. ... women, in particular, have felt the force of these norms.[5]

Thus we can see that an extrovert finds the conflict that is always present in a church more difficult to deal with, as they are often the focus of that conflict.

> In the accounts of pastors faced with congregational conflicts, two themes came up again and again. One was that churches, even those that say they want to grow, are unwilling to make the changes necessary to do it ... A second recurrent theme is an assumption that if there's a conflict in the church, the pastor must somehow be at fault.[6]

If some of the congregation stop talking to me, I have to work hard to keep buoyant despite their behaviour.

33

The Enneagram

This tool for self-understanding grows increasingly popular among Christians, as well as other people. The Enneagram was publicized through the publication of *In Search of the Miraculous* by P. D. Ouspensky, a student of G. I. Gurdjieff, the 'guru' of the Enneagram in 1947. It was presented as a method of increasing self-knowledge, and has now evolved into a personality typing tool, examining our emotional engagement with life. Through the 1950s to 1970s, various people worked on the Enneagram, and it came to Berkeley in California, where various people expanded their understanding of the system, publishing as they went along. The Enneagram is now taught through a workshop scenario, and many people have great respect for it as a useful insight into the way that we function with each other, and how we filter our individual world view.

According to the Enneagram, we have one of nine personality types: Reformer, Helper, Achiever, Individualist, Investigator, Loyalist, Enthusiast, Challenger or Peacemaker. Your type is fixed by the age of about five, and has come about through many factors – genetic, environmental and relational to mention but a few. While the type is fixed, the benefit of the Enneagram is in telling one what behaviour we can work on and so become more content within ourselves. There are also connections across the nine types, aiding a deeper self-understanding.

The Enneagram Institute's website[7] claims the system has been scientifically validated, but Rebecca Nye questions the system's validity:

> Other tests, such as the Enneagram, state things in a way that readily amplifies the more interpretive, quasi-religious, style of reading between the lines for meaning. However, users of this should be aware that its way of

picturing personality lacks any psychological support for its reliability as a scientific measure – it has not been tested against other measures or validated by any external tests.[8]

Dr Nye is someone for whom I have great respect. Her position on the Enneagram remains the same.

In contrast to Dr Nye, there are others within the Church who run courses or have experienced the Enneagram and testify to its benefit in their lives. One such colleague describes it as a useful tool for growth, especially with reference to spiritual growth and development. She likes the way that the Enneagram doesn't dictate to a person, but gives the individual knowledge about their 'normal' way of reacting to different stimuli, enabling the individual to concentrate on the more helpful side of their behaviour. She says that while she knows which type she is, she observes herself switching into different types according to workload and personal stress, and recognizing that behaviour helps her to deal with it in a constructive way. The workshops are facilitated with time for listening and reflection with people who have experience of using the Enneagram, so you can see how to develop the experience on your own. My colleague particularly has benefited from the insight that the Enneagram has given her into group dynamics, and managing groups of people.

Recognizing how we act, and how others can 'rub us up the wrong way' or 'press buttons' is always helpful knowledge, and if the Enneagram lifts the shutters for folk, then it is worth employing as a starter, and those who have found it useful can testify to its power of self-understanding. As a tool for self-knowledge, many people would place the Enneagram beside Myers–Briggs as a useful piece of 'kit' to have in a minister's management toolbox.

Learning styles

As the years go by, more and more differences in how people function are being noted, with tools devised to help us understand our differences. A factor that I encountered about the same time as Myers–Briggs entered my life was that of learning styles. The basic types of learning styles are Activist, Reflector, Theorist and Pragmatist.

Activists are people who like a challenge, they think variety is the spice of life, hope that learning is going to be enjoyable and don't mind making mistakes. Activists bore quickly and 'turn off'. Activists can be quite difficult/challenging people to have in a group, as they will want it to move along at a good pace. They will have an extrovert personality. An activist will approach learning with these questions:

- Will I learn something new?
- I do not want to sit for hours at a time doing nothing. Will there be a mixture of things to do?
- Will I be tied down to one particular subject or method, or are there options?
- Will there be some tough challenges for me to meet so I do not feel as if I am wasting my time?
- Will there be people like me on the course?

Reflectors don't like pressure or being in the spotlight. They may not be good at giving instant responses to groups or exercises, as they like to hear other people's views. They will have an introvert personality. A reflector will approach learning with these questions:

- Will I be given time to prepare and think things through properly or will I be put on the spot?

- Will there be a chance to do things properly, getting relevant information and thinking things out as we go along, or will it be all slap dash?
- Will we be steamrollered along a particular line, not encouraged to think for ourselves but be given answers and information we have no opportunity to question?
- Will I get a chance to hear views of others in the group?
- If I am working alone, will I get enough time to do things properly? Do I have the support and encouragement of anyone outside the course?

Theorists like being intellectually stretched and thrive on argument and discussion. They want to explore the structure of things, the theoretical base and the thinking behind taken for granted assumptions. They may be either extrovert or introvert. A theorist will approach learning with these questions:

- Will I have a chance to question what's going on?
- Does the leaflet in front of me or the tutor of the course have a clear idea of what we are going to learn, how we are going to learn it and why?
- Is this course going to be too easy for me? Or will I only encounter ideas and arguments with which I am already familiar?
- Will there be people with my interests and approach there?

Pragmatists are likely to learn from successful people who have proved their competency in the field rather than from ivory towered experts. Again, they may be either extrovert or introvert. A pragmatist will approach learning with these questions:

- Will there be lots of practical tips and techniques?

- Will there be opportunities to practise?
- Have the people running the course shown that they know how to do this themselves?
- Is this course or event tackling real problems and some of my current concerns?

Within one of my ministry teams, we had an Activist (me), a Reflector (the curate) and two Pragmatists (the readers). Knowing about learning styles helped us to work together in a sensitive and collaborative manner. We were all aware that the Activist and the Reflector can rub each other up the wrong way in their contrasting styles, so all the styles were incorporated in the work that we did together. It's worth noticing that Activists are often extroverts and Reflectors are often introverts. Generally, there are fewer Activist learners in the clergy – it's the type that least suits academic work and most of the clergy are trained through university-style colleges and courses, although that is beginning to change (note the high number of bishops who are 'Oxbridge').

Spiritual styles

Recently arrived in this arena are the Spiritual Styles devised by Joyce Bellous, David Csinos and Denise Peltomaki:[9]

> Spiritual Styles measure the way people express what they are most concerned about. This assessment clarifies what people focus on as they try to make meaning out of life experiences or carry out daily tasks. This assessment offers an opportunity to see how people relate to and express what really matters to them. It also reveals that people have different ways of expressing what matters. Spiritual Styles measure the way we try to improve a situation or make the world a better place.[10]

The styles analyse how an individual interacts with the world, looking at the driving from within, that we find it hard to explain to another. There are four styles: Word, Emotion, Symbol and Action.

Word people use language to make sense of the world. They tend to be 'left brain' oriented. Many academics favour this style, and so this is also common in ordained clergy. They will be accurate, precise and rational.

Emotion people are predominantly 'right brain' thinkers. These people tend to be caring, empathetic, warm, relational and intuitive. As they can be charismatic leaders, Emotion-style people need to be self-aware as they have the potential to cause havoc in organizations such as churches.

Symbol people are quiet, mystic and reflective. They are often solitary and will choose to be meditative. Hermits are the ultimate of this style. Few Symbol people will be at home in church, as it is too constraining for their way of being.

Action people are direct and driven. They can be single minded and want to get things done. A typical Action person works for an non-governmental organization and is passionate about changing the world. Every church needs at least one, to ensure that things do actually happen, although they are often impatient in meetings as the meeting follows procedure and seemingly gets caught up in 'red tape'.

Most people are an amalgam of the four, with one predominant. Ideally, clergy will have a balance of the four styles, but the predominant style in Anglican clergy is Word. As with the other typing tools, people are not fixed in their Spiritual Styles. Many children are Action, wanting to help charities and to affect the world that they live in. By the time they go to college, many have changed their style and have lost the need to change the world in the way that they did when they were at primary school.

Indeed, few children are Symbol dominant – this style develops as you grow older in the same way that personalities move on the Myers–Briggs spectrum towards their shadow as we move through life. How one's Spiritual Style changes as faith grows is a piece of work as yet to be undertaken.

At the time of writing, few people have come across the Spiritual Styles. I personally have found it fascinating, as the type of church that you favour will vary according to your style. For example, if you are an Action person, you will find a church that has a social agenda such as the Salvation Army. Word people like a more didactic style of preaching, while Emotion people get lost in the story and images. Symbol people rarely find church attractive, preferring to go off alone to commune with nature. The Society of Friends is the nearest the Christian church has to a Symbolic style of worship, although even they talk too much for some Symbol people. If someone is within the church and they have a high Symbol value, chances are it will be the Catholic or Orthodox wing.

A blueprint for a typical minister

Thus a 'typical' member of the clergy is probably an introvert, a Reflective or Theorist learner and Word spiritual style. People who share those types will find it easy to relate to that archetypal member of the clergy, but people with other factors will not. Thus, take an Extrovert Activist with an Emotion style and you may have a glimpse of a member of the clergy who is often told they are very unusual – 'not like a vicar at all'. Self-knowledge has helped me to realize that, actually, the way I work isn't like a typical member of the clergy – quite right! But that also means that this type of clergy person feels themselves 'odd' at gatherings of clergy, through no fault of their own or anyone else's, but simply being out of the predominant styles of thinking and being can make you feel quite isolated and 'wrong' in some profound way. Knowing why I feel odd in these gatherings has been enormously helpful. It helps me to recognize that 'it's okay to be me', and relish the wide variety of people within the ordained clergy and the wider church. I could have done with this knowledge many years ago.

The other people who would be helped by this knowledge is the congregation and the people who are working with the clergy, such as in a PCC. The more self-understanding we can get, the more we can stand back from ourselves and reflect on what the dynamic is, and where it came from, without attributing guilt. I was at a writer's conference recently – we were working on some liturgy together. One of the other writers kept saying that she thought my ideas 'wouldn't work in her church', I felt got at, and it all felt very negative. Then I stopped and thought about Spiritual Styles – hers was clearly Word, mine is Emotion, and they are the two that find it hardest to work collaboratively. And suddenly, the personal agenda that I'd brought vanished, and I realized that this may be uncomfortable, but between the two of us, a much better piece of work was being done. No-one was in the right or wrong, and neither was anyone better – simply different. And suddenly it was all so much easier.

That is what a comprehension of group dynamics, personality types, learning preferences and Spiritual Styles can bring when you bring all that knowledge to bear. How many areas of conflict could clergy analyse with these skills? I would like to see all these areas high on the curriculum for ordination training as soon as is possible, for the sake of those being ordained as well as the churches where they will exercise their ministries.

CHAPTER 4
Theological training

What is taught at theological college?

I trained for ministry at St John's Theological College, in Nottingham. The choice of where to go was simple: we lived in Nottingham, my children were at nursery school just around the corner, (state provided, very good, half day every day), and I couldn't see any advantage in moving house, schools etc, for 2 years at college, with more moving house, schools, etc. at the end of the college years.

Prior to the choice of college, there had been another decision to make, as Nottingham also houses a part-time ministry course, based at the University of Nottingham. But the part-time course lasts 3 years, and because I was 30+ by now, full-time training was only 2 years long. That took us to the year that my son started school full time. Add on the fact that by now my husband was commuting to London 3 or 4 days of the week, and hopefully I could aim for a curacy within easier reach of the smoke: in the end the decision was based on what was going to be best for the family, rather than looking at the difference in the types of training available.

Another important factor was that the 'chaps', who were on the whole going on to full-time stipendiary (i.e. with income provided alongside the vicarage) tended to train on the college courses while the women, many of whom were going to be part time and frequently unpaid, trained on the courses. This is no longer as true as it was 20 years ago. But I was aiming to be a vicar in the days when few women were, so I wanted as good a training as the chaps were getting. And there was a value judgement there; at the time, there was more credence given to full-time training. It was going to be hard enough as a woman to get a full-time curacy without the hint that my training was perceived as somehow inferior.

I trained from 1990 until 1992. Bells may be ringing – I completed my college training in the June and General Synod agreed to the ordination of women to the priesthood in the following November. This meant that when I left college to be ordained deacon (as everyone is) I didn't know if I would ever get to be a priest. This had been helpful at the time of my application for ordination, as I needed to support of the Church which we attended week by week, and the vicar there (who, at the time of writing, is one of the 'flying bishops')[1] was, and is still, very much opposed to women priests. He would not have supported an application for priesthood, but had no qualms about women as deacons. I have to add at that I didn't know if I wanted to be a priest at this point – I just felt called to work within the Church.

I trained with a group of men. I was the only female ordinand (someone who has been recommended for ordination by the selection group that operates on behalf of the bishops) that year at my college. There were women above me, and there would be women in the year below, and there were others who were studying for other qualifications, but being the only woman ordinand in the year group was a bit daunting. I was fairly feminist in my views at that time, (age brought about some mellowing, but I'm still quite scary for some people) so had a difficult time with some of the more conservative evangelicals, especially among the wives of my colleagues, some of who told me they thought I should be at home looking after my children.

I benefited enormously from the many excellent aspects of my training and loved my placements. The weekly sermon class in the second year was very well taught, and I enjoyed the mix of chaps (and female as well as male lecturers) that I worked alongside. I enjoyed writing many of the essays. My passion for children's spirituality was kick-started in working alongside Howard Worsley with the children in college, and I was used by other students as a sounding board and compassionate listener, which sowed the seeds of the spiritual direction that I now engage with. The spirituality mornings were interesting and foundational for my later work. The training was broad, and college introduced me to the type of people who I would be working with over the next years. Many had relocated to train, and we were a very mixed bunch, but all driven by the certainly that we had been called to minister – that we had a vocation.

As a person who is an Activist learner, the apprenticeship style of training, experienced as placements, suited me well, occurring in the work that we did out of the college. Throw in the Christmas review, being student vice-president in my second year and running the college drama group – it was a mixed education that I mainly enjoyed, and sometimes endured. The most important aspect for me was the relationships, and many of those are still in place.

We did little, if anything, about the day-to-day logistics of parish life. I later joked that working a tea urn should be number one lesson, closely followed by a crash course in accounting, chairing meetings and managing volunteers (often alluded to as 'herding cats'). These areas were supposed to be covered during the curacy – the first post in ministry after training, but it depended on your training vicar as to how well these areas were covered. In the subsequent 18 years since I left college, the training has moved on, and the colleges and local courses that

I spoke to during my research had some variation around the core curriculum, responding to the needs of the students in each college.

The need of the Church to economize as much as possible, alongside the steady increase in the average age of an ordinand (from 32 when I was ordained to around 50 at the time of writing) means that the courses are growing increasingly popular as attempts are made to streamline the system. Courses are also more diverse in the type of ministry that they train for. Many ordinands are now offering themselves after early retirement or redundancy, and these people are less deployable, as families and partners' working lives fix a family into an area. Others need to fit their ministry around a professional spouse who may not be able to move location or children who are in secondary education, for whom moving schools can prove a nightmare. (We moved from a comprehensive to grammar school area half way through my daughter's GCSE course and ended up putting her into private education for a year – the local grammar schools were all full. Good job my husbands' income could fund it).

Courses still run for 3 years, and many who have used these courses speak highly of the experience. The extra year makes for a better focus on the here and now. The fact that students remain in the family home is good for their budgets as well as reducing stress levels associated with two relocations for college (one at the beginning, another at the end). Tutors who work on the courses speak of the critical second year as one where ordinands begin to orientate themselves towards ministry, in a way that cannot happen in the 2 years usually undertaken at a college. Alongside, as the courses are regional, they don't tend to have such a dominant churchmanship as the college, and so the students can examine different churchmanships from their own in a more secure environment, and 'cherry pick' or even move in their appreciation of other styles and types of worship. Local churches can support their ordinands in a very concrete way, and there is no need for families to relocate for training – all big financial savings as well as removing the stress of making friends and finding support in what can be a very difficult time for family members.

In the area where I now live (Canterbury/Rochester diocesan border) we have many people training for ordained local ministry in Canterbury diocese[2], which means they stay in the church where they have worshipped since before ordination. Their training is thorough and involves placements, but the idea is that they return whence they came and contribute to the community there. Few, if any, receive payment for this ministry.

There are self-supporting ministers (also called non-stipendiary ministers or NSMs) right across the country, who work as many hours for the local church as they have negotiated for expenses only, and frequently not claiming those expenses. Many of these self-supporting ministers are women or retired men.

Fairly new to the Church of England is the role of 'pioneer ministry'. Trained alongside their parish intended colleagues, they have been selected to work in a different environment – that of an area of life where the Church may not have much presence, such as night clubs. They may be stipendiary or not, depending on how they have felt called. At present, there are few such ministers, and the Church is watching to see how much effect they have.

In virtually all English dioceses, there are systems for several types of lay (non-ordained) ministry, each with their own specific training. These people are nearly always offering this ministry part time, often holding down a full-time job as well.

In the ordained ministry, all the archdeacons that I spoke to in the course of my research commented that there are more factors coming into play with clergy deployment. A theological college lecturer reflected that there is no longer the understanding that being a minister involves sacrifice (for example, one of their recently trained ministers asked for Christmas off to go away with their family). Factors such as the spouse's job, often giving more income than the minister's, whether children could easily move schools, what the schools were like and if the family even want to live in this area are now causing 'problems' in deploying newly ordained clergy. This is illustrated by several ordinands who had trained at Wycliffe college, Oxford, (which has a strongly evangelical slant), who turned down posts rather than be employed within a church that did not suit their 'churchmanship' in 2009. Certainly, Savage and Boyd-Macmillan comment;

> Last year, in a class of 50 trainee ministers, we asked how many of the trainees had been 'sent out' from thriving, growing churches. Around 80% raised their hands. We then did the maths on the whiteboard to estimate the probability of serving, after their training, in a thriving, growing church in the UK (given the number of trainees seeking posts, the number of posts and the number of growing churches in the country). Our estimate was that each trainee had a 1 in 400 chance of serving in a growing, thriving church. How many still believed that they would be the one lucky, blessed person to get the thriving post? Around 80% of the class again raised their hands. Even when we have done the maths, we still think the probabilities do not apply to us ... Disappointment is the result.[3]

Many curates struggle in their posts, finding what they expected is far from what they are living with. In *Public People,*

Private Lives by Jean and Chris Burton,[4] the plight of many curates is discussed and it's not a happy read. Likewise the attitudes reflected in the 'management group' used by the Burtons pick up on the seeming gap between the curates and the archdeacons that I found in my research.

Many curates end up in a course of counselling during their time as curate. Issues can emerge, not always to do with the Church, and I was encouraged at one of the theological colleges that I visited to discover that the warden finds money from the budget to get the pre-emptive counselling in during the training, when the huge support of communal living is in place and you are living with people in a similar place in their lives, rather than during the curacy. The warden at that college was involved in training curates in her previous post, and so knows what can happen during the curacy period.

The colleges and courses all work under very tight criteria and budgets, with a curriculum that is largely set through the central church. Many ordinands at college are only there for 2 years, so time is tight to help these amazingly good people to recognize what they need to learn and take on board before they re-enter the church with their collars turned around. Because it is impossible to realize what vicarage life is like if you haven't lived in one, some of the moans and groans that you hear at college seem strange and unconnected with the central vocation that drives all in such a place. In reality, many ordinands are often only focussed on college for the first year, as by the beginning of the second they are looking for that curacy, and many will know not only the church to which they will be moving by the middle of their second year (usually leaving in early June for an end-of-month ordination and the curacy beginning) but the house which they will be occupying. They could fail the course, but that is exceptionally rare if they do the work required, so 99.9

per cent will have their eyes firmly fixed on the last essay deadline of the second year. As one of the lecturers that I spoke to said:

> Some people are just too deeply entrenched in their own ideas about church to be changed as we feel they may need changing, or at least opening up. There is a process, a syllabus; both with intended outcomes, but 'some people just hold their breath'.

The process of theological training includes 'formation': a sense of being who you are – that God called you and is with you through all the changes of life. Formation involves a need to get hold of a sense of purpose, vision and direction, which is seen in small steps of progress, and a need for a familiarity with the institution of Church (that many ordinands do not have), to lower the shock factor when they encounter it – many returning curates confess 'I wish I'd listened more closely'.

I was encouraged by the quality of the teaching that courses and colleges give, and the dedication of the staff as they equip people for the challenging life that they are preparing to take up.

Are we training the right people?

All ordinands come from their own specific church, which it is easy to assume is 'the pattern' for the Church. Sadly, it is not, as every church is different from every other. What the curate encounters may be deeply disappointing, through no fault of the training parish.

As previously stated, many clergy have introverted personality types, and are often Word oriented in their spiritual style. Perhaps we should actively look for a wider spread of personality and spiritual types, to meet the need of differing types of churches. Once ordinands are through the selection process, it takes a brave theological educator to ring alarm bells about someone, but it is evident that those bells do need to ring more often.

There is a drive at the moment to recruit younger people for ordination. The reasons for this are largely self-evident:

- It costs a lot to train a minister, so the longer they can serve, the better value for money.
- Older curates rarely have enough experience to become senior clergy, such as archdeacons or bishops.
- The congregation often mirrors the age of the minister – so older ministers bring in an older congregation.
- Younger clergy have a better understanding of how younger people 'work' and so can communicate far more effectively.
  The negatives for younger clergy are:
- The congregation may well regard them as 'wet behind the ears' and not respond well to their ministry.
- They may find it harder to relate to the older members of the church in their worship needs.
- Younger members of the church may have difficulties maintaining boundaries.

Many of the younger ordinands come from successful city churches and will have had little experience of rural ministry or life. Good training placements can work wonders here, but younger curates will frequently look for a parish which is urban rather than rural. And few rural parishes have the luxury of a curacy being based at their church(es).

Is the training serving the ordinands well? This is difficult to answer, as training builds on life experience which is always individual. The profound question of whether clergy are able to speak effectively to congregations (especially children and young people) is questioned by Griffiths:

> There has been a significant shift in the way children
> learn; therefore there must be a significant shift in the
> way the Children's Outreach Projects communicate ...
> This inability to communicate effectively, particularly in
> understanding the power of narrative, will ultimately lead
> to further decline. It is imperative that those who speak
> in Children's Outreach Projects ... become students of
> public speaking, giving time to understand the subtleties
> of communication today.[5]

Take out 'Children's Outreach Projects' and insert 'the Church'
and you have a realization that our clergy training needs to
understand the way that life really has moved on and that those
of us who aren't up to speed with technology need to be fast-
tracked in those skills. It seems that they may hold one of the
keys to attracting and keeping children, young people and 'young
families' in church – one of the criteria seen in many clergy
person specifications used for advertising such posts. And, of
course, children and young people are part of the church today,
and as we oldies fall off the perch, will become the Church per
se. Lewis and Lewis add:

> ... the cultural communications revolution is aiming
> people in another direction. Today's visual communica-
> tions are retraining our minds. For the first time in half
> a millennium the right side of the brain is clamouring
> for prominence and insisting on involvement in life and
> learning.[6]

The implication of this comment is that perhaps we should look
for more 'right brain' thinkers in the ministry; probably N in
Myers–Briggs terms, and Emotion or Symbol in their spiritual

style. Needless to say, these are in the minority at the moment. Such people are naturally creative, and bringing such creativity into liturgy and worship can be uncomfortable for those who operate in a Word manner. (Such as the liturgical committee of General Synod, who write the worship that Anglican clergy use.)

Understanding the thinking shift is important, along with helping elderly congregations to appreciate the need for them making space to accommodate other ways of worshipping that will be more appropriate to our multi-tasking younger people. While this is easier for the younger curates and clergy, the many older ordinands may struggle with new forms of media being used to present the gospel, and the multi-tasking, multi-media lifestyle of many younger people today.

How could we better equip clergy?

With the advantage of hindsight, there are various areas of training that would have helped me be a better minister earlier on in my parish life. They are all areas of knowledge that I acquired on my journey through 16 years of life in the vicarage. For me, self-knowledge is key, coupled with an understanding of the social psychology of group behaviour.

In the previous chapter, we discussed various psychological tools that are now widely available. Myers–Briggs is now taught at every college and course, usually quite early on, to help ordinands who haven't used the type to more self-knowledge. Learning styles may also be taught, possibly part of an early study skills series of hints and tips to help mature students as they knuckle down once again to researching and writing. At the time of writing, it appears that Spiritual Styles has yet to reach the curriculum.

Continuing ministerial education

All clergy have to continue training after their ordination: continuing ministerial education (CME), colloquially referred to as potty training (post-ordination training) is obligatory for 4 years in most dioceses. What is taught on these courses varies from diocese to diocese, but designed to augment what is going on in the parish, helping curates to reflect critically and theologically on their experiences and lives together. Many curates resent the work and the intrusion into their ministry, and traditionally take out all their angst on their situation within this context, which can make it a very difficult process for those trying to hold it together. Many dioceses now teach CME to Masters level. This may be problematic for the less academic curates, for whom training may have been quite a struggle, despite the fact that they may be brilliant on the ground. Essays may be flexible in presentation, from the 4,000 words on paper to a website/interactive piece of work, and the providers work hard to make the courses relevant and of a high standard. The awful fact is that some clergy leave CME as soon as they can, and only occasionally engage with any further training in their ensuing ministry.

Key knowledge that I was taught on CME is an understanding of faith development for which Fowler and Westerhoff are the most commonly used names. Over the last 50 years, academics have been working at the concept of faith and trying to make schemes of how faith grows in human beings. Both Fowler and Westerhoff have worked and written extensively in this field and come up with systems that help us to understand and recognize the changes and development in the faith that we share with those among whom we live and work. Both recognize that their work has produced tools to give insight. Neither would claim that these schemes are perfect and both recognize that many people do not easily fit the potential boxes that the schemes give us. Both are American, but the schemes are applicable to those people within the developed world who live in what are, or were, broadly Christian societies. The insight that these theories give will ring true in many cases; but it must always be born in mind that these theories are not proven fact. They are tools to help us understand the processes of a person's spiritual development.

It is important to note that Fowler and Westerhoff use the word 'faith' as a psychological construct in their definitions and theories rather then as a theological term. Faith, in Fowler's terms, is an internal concept to which we attach great importance in our understanding of who we are as individuals. He states that all people have faith, although it may not be religious – he speaks of faith as a recognition that there is more to life than just the physical and while that may involve belief in the transcendent, that may not be what you or I would name as 'God'. If our faith involves trust and a loyalty towards that transcendent being so that we develop religious faith, then we will indeed speak of 'God' and having faith in that God. Fowler's assertion that all people have faith is widely held among people working in the fields of faith development or spirituality. Westerhoff, says that faith is the internal, dynamic belief, while religion is the expression of that belief and that there is a clear differential between the two. He continues that faith is deeply personal, a living, growing belief: Westerhoff would say that my religion is how I express my belief held within.

Both Fowler and Westerhoff have developed schemes of faith development, which do not always agree in how they function, but of which a basic awareness gives enormous benefit to a member of the clergy as they analyse how their flock is moving on spiritually. Faith and spirituality are the grit and grist of a clergy person's teaching role, but if we don't know how to recognize where folk are in their journey, how can we support and facilitate movement through the more difficult points of life?

There are still many members of the clergy who are ignorant of these theories and others who reject them, perhaps because they can challenge those of us who are supposed to know about such things. In *One Generation From Extinction* by Mark Griffiths,[7] a book that examines the work of unchurched children's groups within local churches, he examines the teaching that the children receive, and reflects that knowledge of Fowler would ensure that this was more apposite for the needs of these children. I would add that the knowledge would also enable clergy in their work with adults. Certainly, Fowler's theories may present more challenges for some in the evangelical wing of the church, but knowledge would help clergy understand how communication of the good news may need to be nuanced according to the listeners.

It was during my MA[8] (commenced 6 years into parish ministry) that I engaged with social psychology and group theory and analysed what was causing great stress in my life – the differing expectations of my two churches and their congregations. Until then I had looked at psychology from time to time, but the dynamics of a group proved essential knowledge not only to my sanity, but to working with two churches in managing their expectations. Okay, this angel Gabriel lost her wings a long time ago, but that is what parishes look for!

I also had the benefit of a churchwarden with an MBA, who would quietly coach me in the kindest way when people were proving intractable as to how to get that elusive 'win–win' conclusion.

Theological college is not adequate to give everyone an MBA, but training in how people work and function is essential – perhaps as part of the CME that curates have to take part in.

There is also a need for ordinands to recognize the reality of what many parish churches are like. Curacies usually take place in larger parishes, to cover the range of activities that the curate must learn about, but the following first incumbency may be at a village, or more likely several villages, where there are many meetings, differing expectations and where there may be lay folk who've effectively run the place for years. And they may well have needed to, as clergy posts grow larger and larger, with more administration for the lay people to accommodate if it is to be done. Or perhaps at a small town church, where life is tough and few people come to church week by week, but the demands for the occasional offices (especially funerals) may be enormous and very draining of energy. Or they may find themselves in a run-down urban parish, where there are few able people to help with the increasingly complicated parish administration and no money to pay for it. The addition of vicarage burglaries and vandalism can be the last straw for a struggling clergyperson. One area of Nottingham was known for the terrible effects it had on the mental health of the succession of vicars and their families. Helping clergy to effect change in a church is a critical skill and one that few of my experience have been taught.

Time management appears on the curriculum usually towards the end of a college training or course, and everyone nods their heads wisely. The Burtons reflect that maybe all clergy need to take note of these sessions:

> Many of the issues that concerned the curates related to absence of boundaries, particularly in four areas: responsibility; communication; time management and the place of the family; and working from home.[9]

Undertaking work–life balance workshops for clergy tells me

that few remember the wise words that they heard at college. Boundaries and how to create them and hold onto them is a critical part of a parish clergy person's being able to flourish. An archdeacon that I spoke to described how over the course of his years in the parish, he put together a system for 'flourishing' which largely involved keep boundaries carefully, via good use of an answerphone, a wife who could take a day off mid-week, and being strict with himself. Few clergy talk of themselves as 'flourishing': 'surviving' is more commonly heard. Time management is key to successful parish ministry, or the minister will crash and burn, taking early retirement on health grounds, as many do every year.

The other big area that I feel is missing now is one that has only 'arrived' in the last 15 years – that of children's spirituality. This area of study was kick-started by David Hay and Rebecca Nye in their study of children in Nottinghamshire which they wrote about in *The Spirit of the Child*.[10] This key book formed the basis of much subsequent work and tells us much about the inherent spirituality which we share as adults – for we have all been children. All clergy come into contact with children, so it seems obvious to me that clergy need specific training on child development and spirituality. But it remains an optional extra at many courses and colleges, and 'Family' or 'All age' services remain painful to observe when led by well meaning clergy who don't have a clue about how to relate to small people, or the alienating (and so boring) effects of the 'jargon'[11] that Anglican liturgies often employ. An understanding of child spirituality will shed light on much of adult spirituality and so facilitate good small group work as well as preaching and teaching generally.

Once clergy are free of compulsory CME (4 years after ordination), attendance at such events is voluntary. While chapter meetings may include elements of CME, many clergy find their diaries too full to get to a regular training session, a regular retreat or even a day off. This is often purely down to poor boundaries and a feeling of being the only person who can do this task. Even if that is true, ongoing training and support is critical if parish clergy are to manage their work load and thrive as individuals. As mentioned previously, there is an evident need for clergy to be up to speed with new technologies, and in-service training could be provided by other clergy who have a good understanding in the field.

Are we selecting the 'right people' for the task?

In my conversations, the same sort of expression kept cropping up. People need to have a clear sense of vocation, with an independence from the psychological strokes that the institution gives. They also have to work for many years without a career structure – although some incumbencies are perceived as 'desirable', very few will become archdeacons or bishops.

Clergy need to have a very secure sense of themselves in order to cope with the expectation and criticism that they will receive in their work (and that criticism can extend to their spouse and children):

> What became increasingly significant ... was the second command, implied or directly given to all families by all levels of the church and community, that 'the job must come first'.[12]

The teenagers in particular spoke very strongly about expectations of them in many aspects of their lives, both from church members and from contemporaries. The 'unwritten contract' of the job for them, as well as their parents, could be very difficult to handle. The impression was that families felt they were negotiating a minefield.[13]

People need to be secure within themselves if they are to function as both priest and prophet – as more than just a chaplain to the congregation. A sense of vocation is critical – have you got the 'oomph' that doesn't need to be needed? Warren comments that in her interviews for her work[14] that many of the interviewees were people who needed to feel needed. She also reflects that those who volunteered to take part in her study may well have been those who had an 'axe to grind' and that many were displaying symptoms of depression. Her report is not a cheerful read, and neither is the Burton's.

Savage and Boyd-Macmillan make some interesting comments about the sort of person that colleges and courses train, and that parishes look for:

> The individualistic, competitive educational process that trainee ministers undergo tends to churn out newly minted leaders as loners, 'one man bands'. This is so despite the current approbation for empowering leaders. ... While many churches today talk a good talk about leadership (servant leaders, empowering leaders, shared leadership), secretly, many churches continue to want a Great Leader to lead them to the Promised Land where they won't have any more problems. ... Another expression is seen in the widespread desire for a minister with a perfect nuclear family ... The most desired template for a Protestant parish priest is one with a young family.[15]

When the bishop rang to tell me that I hadn't been chosen for one post, he added, somewhat ruefully, 'He had a baby, Ronni

...'. I had had two teenagers and hadn't taken my husband on the interview. The successful candidate had taken his rather delightful wife. Am I bitter? Well, that's life in the Church of England, and if I'd got that post I wouldn't have got St Somewhere, which I really enjoyed.

With the rising age of ordinands, the Church now has within her ranks people with diverse and very valuable life and work experience. The problem is that they may only be vicar of one parish before retirement. Many parishes are wary of taking a first-time incumbent even if they are 50+, and make assumptions about capability without realizing that someone who was, maybe, a consultant surgeon in her previous life will bring all sorts of skills that 20 years in a parish may not have supplied. Such people nearly always train on the courses, as they are far cheaper, and if the minister only has perhaps 15 years on parish work left – you have to cut your cloth ... Thus the number of people attending the colleges is shrinking, and becoming less diverse in the major centres of Oxford and Cambridge. (This is not as true for the more 'scattered' colleges such as Durham or Bristol.)

The problem that increasing age brings is not quality, but of the limiting of experience that will make the pool from which archdeacons and bishops are appointment shrink rapidly. At the time of writing, bishops still have to be men, but fewer and fewer have been in ministry for long enough to have the knowledge and life experience that is critical for a good bishop. That problem is going to get worse rapidly in the next few years if the Church doesn't bite the bullet about women as bishops. That will only help a little, as the age of women offering for ministry has always been quite a high average, as most women traditionally wait for their children to be independent before offering for ministry selection.

The Church will never get it completely right, but my fear is that we are trailing in our training, and successive budget cuts are not going to help the church to really re-engage with the people we live among, and for so many of whom we are largely irrelevant.

CHAPTER 5
Support for clergy

Many clergy claim that they feel unsupported in their ministry. Bishops can seem far away, archdeacons may be more associated with a breakdown or failure (rather as the villain, as portrayed in the BBC 2010 comedy *Rev*). This feeling is always subjective, but stories of how long you can wait to see senior management abound, and it was certainly true for me in my last diocese (6 weeks approximately for non-urgent business with the bishop). Bishops have 'emergency' slots in their diary, but to ask for one of these slots is to admit that you've got a problem. I used one such slot when I was in St Elsewhere's diocese, and the bishop was excellent, but by that time we all knew that I had a problem in the parish. This diary squeeze reflects the workloads of bishops, but that is beyond the scope of this book. So what support do clergy have, and how much do they access that support?

Cell groups

Clergy who belong to cell groups often cite them as their best support. These groups are self-selected, usually at the end of theological training, and they usually meet just once or twice a year, although some are more frequent. Groups often go away together for 24–48 hours, to a retreat house. The agenda is to talk through what is happening in each person's work (and life) and for the others to listen and support. The group holds strict confidence. Clergy who belong to such a group often meet up for many years, sometimes right through the working life, and members return to the parish having been listened to, with their life supported and prayerfully strengthened. Perhaps the most important aspect is that each person is given time and love, in a very genuine form. Because they all trained together, they often arrive at the same transition points together, and can offer real support to each other in a very safe way. This group is completely independent of any other structure, which may be what makes it so safe and helpful.

Chapter

Clergy often cite chapter as the least supportive group! There is a cartoon in the *Church Times* called 'St Gargoyles', and it features the life of the aforementioned church. For many years, I had a 'St Gargoyles' cartoon in my diary; the picture was of the exhausted cleric standing back against the front door. The caption? 'Another day with drunks, dropouts and ne'er do wells; Clergy Chapter'. Cynical, but with elements of truth. Certainly, this reflects Warren's comment:

> Chapter meetings have been notorious for the lack of caring support and for the insidious competitiveness that is generated.[1]

In my experience, chapters are unlike any other type of meeting. As a woman member of chapter I found myself befriending new women to the area, but as someone recently arriving in a new chapter, I found the inability of the other clergy to place exactly what I now do alienated them for quite a while. My experience in the chapters I have belonged to has been of a slightly competitive place, where clergy found it very hard to be honest about their work. The slight unease between clergy from different churchmanship, the inability of some to even talk to women priests and the very busy-ness of clergy life excluded much support. My best experience was in St Somewhere's diocese, where the local chapter had an annual 'booze cruise' to a retreat house near Boulogne. We would have lunch (three courses), a social time, set the funeral fees for the coming year and sometimes have some training input, then hit Cite Europe. All in a day! It was great – and the French wine we had with lunch (included in the cost) undoubtedly helped it all along. Travelling in two or three cars meant we chatted and laughed through the journey. Enforced time in close proximity worked well. One or two of the chapter never came – one even said he only came to 'meetings with an agenda'. It was his loss.

Chapters depend so much on the make up of the local clergy, which changes regularly, and the personality of the person in nominal charge – the area or rural dean. Again, the best one I ever had was in the same chapter mentioned above, where one area dean had the most brilliant sense of humour. When he was chapter clerk, the minutes of meetings were full of puns that made me laugh out loud. Not often you can say that. But it made a huge difference, and I was very sorry when he stood down. His personality affected the whole group in a very positive way. Whether chapter is supportive depends so much on how the individuals interact, and that is not predictable. And I have no doubt that for the clergy who have problems with ordaining women, the advent of people like me made the meetings far more problematic.

Archdeaconries
Most dioceses have two or three archdeacons, who have been promoted from within parish ministry, and each of those is in charge of a geographical area, which will contain many deaneries, with their clergy chapters. How supportive the

archdeacon is again depends on personality. I have worked under one archdeacon that would just drop in, leaving a card to say you'd missed him. As he often dropped by at school-run time, we never actually sat down in a one-to-one conversation. Another was 'book to see' on my initiative. The next ran the local appraisal scheme for the bishop in his archdeaconry, so everyone saw him at least once every 3 years. This same archdeacon also ran training for all his clergy twice a year, which was greatly appreciated by those of us who attended, both for the training and the chance to meet.

A friend described her work as archdeacon as being a carthorse and the bishop is the racehorse. Thus it is usually the archdeacon who arrives when there is a problem of any kind, but the bishop drops in for celebratory services. How much support clergy get from their archdeacon depends on the person-alities involved, and the management style of the archdeacon. Archdeacons are often expected to work wonders by the laity, while actually, if the minister has the freehold (on Appraisal, see below) there could be very little that they can actually achieve.

Bishops

People outside the church have the idea that bishops are at the end of a phone for their clergy. He certainly is on *The Archers*. My experience of bishops is very similar to archdeacons – bishops can be brilliant pastorally, or quite dire: it depends on the man. Most of them have a secretary who sorts out their diary, and a chaplain who does the liturgical leg work, preparing services etc. and making sure that parishes that are being visited are on the ball, Those who are married have a wife who has a strange role to fulfil and they work at that as they see fit. At the time of writing, all bishops are men, but some archdeacons are women.

There is no way of foreseeing how good someone will be as a bishop. Their lives are stuffed with committees and various pieces of administration, and for many it must be a thankless task, with the occasional glow of pleasure at a job done well. (I have heard it said that bishops also suffer from a lack of support.) The present suffragan bishop of St Somewhere is wonderful at licensing services, where a new incumbent arrives, and reflecting very good people skills. My previous bishop of St Elsewhere was an enormously caring man, with a brilliant ability to remember who his clergy were, even if he met you out and about. Yes, there were other areas where he was sometimes criticized, but he was available to see clergy in crisis, and that's not always so in my experience. And the archbishops and their bishops never get it right for everyone – they just can't.

Assisted appraisal

For over 20 years, St Albans diocese has had an optional appraisal scheme for clergy. When I was in that diocese, I joined up as I became an incumbent. Every 4 months or so, I would go and chat to my facilitator, telling her how life was going, and she would feed back. She would see the difference, the progress (or not) and I came away feeling as if I was perhaps making headway. This was an enormously important activity for me, and although I've told others about it, the actual difficulty of recruiting and training the volunteer facilitators seems to have put other dioceses off. I did opt in, and I don't know how many others did, but for me, it was invaluable. Perhaps because I knew that everything that I said would remain within the four walls, and that the person I saw cared about what was happening. A highly skilled professional, the time she gave to me was part of her stewardship to the church. The post I was in at the time was very complicated and demanding, and she certainly helped to keep the stress levels at bay, as well as gently helping me to see the wood through the trees.

Other dioceses have their own versions of this, but for some it involves sharing with other members of the clergy, and at once people are less able to be completely honest as the clergy competitiveness creeps in. The one-to-one nature of the St Albans scheme is its strength, and the clergy-lay mix is very helpful and non-threatening.

Formal appraisal/ministerial development review

There are numerous expectations of a priest and to measure anything of a person's vocation requires a clear idea of what the role and ministry should include. Such ministry demands that the ordained person exemplify an intense spiritual life, filled with those qualities and virtues that are typical of a person who presides over and leads a community. This is an incredible burden to place on one person ... Yet the prevailing assumption is that the minister is, or should be, competent in all areas of ministry.[2]

Previous to 2011, many clergy arrived in the parish to be given the 'freehold', which meant that unless they seriously blotted their copybook, they had the parish until they decided to move on. Great for clergy security, but not so good if they were doing a poor job. There were very few rights for the parish, and the responsibilities laid down in canon law were few. Common tenure, coming in from 2011 (see Appendix 1) lays down rights and responsibilities, and clergy will watch its development with interest. Certainly, it places clergy who don't have freehold in a weaker position, but one great advantage is that parishes now have to specify what they want in their vicar, rather than aim for Archangel Gabriel and see who they get.

With the arrival of common tenure, clergy will be obliged to undergo ministerial development review (MDR) and so be encouraged to undertake specific further training. Most dioceses already have such ministerial reviews, usually every 2 or 3 years for incumbents, but the new arrangements will make it obligatory for all those who no longer hold the freehold to the parish, and highly recommended for those who don't.

As one (suffragan) bishop said to me, this means that the documentation sent to would-be vicars about a parish will have to be far more honest about the skeletons in the cupboard, and it could be just a matter of time before a PCC is sued for misrepresentation of the post. It is usually only after you've arrived in the parish that you learn the truth about why the previous incumbent left, and they rarely share that with the parishioners.

MDR has great potential for helping clergy to address training needs in a constructive manner. Ideally the reviewer will be someone whom the minister trusts and respects, so their recommendations will be helpful and seen as constructive rather than as destructive criticism. One of the main areas of training could be in 'leadership skills':

> Leadership has become a far more critical element in the life and work of a parish priest ... better ways of identifying the particular training and educational needs of the clergy will be required in order for them to provide good leadership and other skills.'[3]

Many lay people criticize the clergy for a lack of 'leadership'. What they mean by that expression is as varied as the people who utter it, but dioceses are ahead of the game with this one, several focussing on leadership skills for curates as well as established clergy. Good training courses, where clergy can share success rather than dwelling on their perceived failures often offer the best sort of support.

A colleague who is at present on a 2-year leadership skill course (several days away at regular intervals) comes back having met with like-minded people, talked about how he is better managing his work–life balance and learning new ways to handle and manage his congregation. This course is across the two Kent dioceses, with shared trainers and a shared skill base. This is a great example of team working that can be copied across the country, and the course duplicated as tired clergy come back with the spring back in their step.

My St Somewhere archdeacon commented to me that most clergy don't need more academic training, but training in praxis – how they apply what they know to what they do. Many feel they lack pastoral skills and are behind the times in their use of modern technology, and all need to be encouraged to cherish their individuality, to be reassured and affirmed in their ministry, to reflect critically with another ordained member of the clergy and to hear affirmation.

The best further training that I undertook was my MA.[4] This was suggested by the bishop at an appraisal session with him. To tell an already harassed clergy person to take on more work sounded absolutely oxymoronic at the time, but it was fantastic! Every week I took out time to think wider than the parish and meet with others who were training for their ministry. This was an ecumenical course, mixing people like me, with several years' ministerial experience, with the ordinands at the colleges. The breadth of the courses that I could choose from meant I could address the gaps in my knowledge and tackle some of the questions from previous experiences that were just sitting at the back of my mind until I was given the space to explore them reflectively through essays and seminars. But this was the wisdom of an experienced bishop, talking to a fairly inexperienced vicar who was struggling – the man was truly wise, with vision that extended way beyond my horizon.

Every diocese has a counselling service available for clergy. However, this takes time and usually asks for some financial contribution. Counselling always requires energy too, as the person works through their discoveries and healing. Not every minister chooses to take this route. MDR could recommend such a course of counselling, but it would be hard to enforce such a recommendation.

The amusingly titled *If You Meet George Herbert On The Road, Kill Him* by Justin Lewis-Anthony encourages clergy to move away from a sixteenth century approach to parochial ministry. Wright follows suit:

> It is significant that as late as the 1950s those writing about the ordained life should still have a model of ordained ministry that would not have been out of place in the sixteenth century.[5]

I think I would change 1950s to twenty-first century. I had parishioners in my last parish who expected me to behave along that pattern; prayer, visiting the parishioners, baptism, marriage, death. The idea of some of the amazing situations that clergy now find themselves in was not on their radar.

What goes wrong?

I can only propose a few ideas of what can go wrong within the parish. From asking five archdeacons, these were the replies to why clergy had left ministry from their archdeaconries (each one different, and reflecting the type of area in their charge): drink, the affair, money and pornography.

As with society as a whole, most clergy drink, and some to excess. For single clergy especially, coming back to an empty vicarage from a meeting that was tough, the easiest way to relax may be to have a stiff drink. My own alcohol consumption was far higher when I was in the parish. Alcoholism is on the increase in the general population, and clergy are not excepted.

Clergy under stress or those for whom the home relationship is not supplying the support they feel they need often resort to a new partner. These 'vicar runs off with curate/organist/ Sunday school teacher' tragedies often hit the national papers. Why clergy resort to affairs is a complicated matter, but they do, and it is a source of great hurt and pain for everyone when it happens. Some parishioners fall in love with their member of the clergy as a matter of course, and that can be very hard to negotiate. Again, clergy are people, and we are not above the usual temptations of life. Marriages fail, and for clergy, that can be very much in the public eye, and excruciatingly difficult to negotiate, even in a 'no fault' situation.

An incumbent's stipend is never that much money, especially for someone who may have been earning far more in their previous life. If the partner is not working, or if there is no partner, the cost of feeding and clothing a family, even when done frugally and with great care can be very difficult to manage. There are charities to help; but …. And living on a single stipend can be very hard, especially if you live in an affluent area.

More men than women view pornography, but apparently the internet is used for more than church websites by some clergy.

Pastors in Transition is a book about ministers in the USA. They list the most common reasons for leaving ministry as:

(i) preference for another kind of ministry; (ii) need to care for children or family; (iii) conflict in the congregation; (iv) conflict with denominational leaders; (v) feelings of burnout or frustration; (vi) sexual misconduct; and (vii) divorce or marital problems.[6] Most of these areas call for careful support and counselling for the minister if they are to remain in their parish and coping. Several of the people who I contacted regarding reasons for leaving ministry cited divorce: for those of a more evangelical stance, the break up of a marriage, even when they were not at fault, was too big an obstacle for their ministry, and they resigned their parishes. Others manage to carry on in the parish, but carrying a heavy load for months or years.

For some women, caring for elderly parents or young children meant that a parish post in the usual manner was unmanageable.[7] I found that people were actually more generous to me as a woman when they called – answering the door in an apron and dog collar is confounding. And parishioners soon learned that I didn't pick up the phone during family meal times, or if I was mid way through cooking. Male colleagues are often plagued at meal times by the phone, as 'I knew you'd be in'. Maybe they shouldn't answer at those times either.

Conflict in the congregation, or with a particular member of the congregation, can wear a minister out:

> One of two main reasons why ministers left parish ministry was the stress of dealing with conflict.[8]
>
> At a clergy conference, a show of hands indicated that 80% of the clergy present found that one of the greatest stressors in their lives was that one *really* difficult person in their congregation.[9]
>
> In the accounts of pastors faced with congregational conflicts, two themes came up again and again. One was

that churches, even those that say they want to grow, are unwilling to make the changes necessary to do it.' [10]

A second recurrent theme is an assumption that if there's a conflict in the church, the pastor must somehow be at fault. [11]

Conflict wears the minister down. Having to regularly act as mediator between two warring families in my last parish required tact, time and energy. I was also working at the ends of my capabilities. The diocese later introduced a professional mediator to do this sort of work, and she was a busy lady. There is also the endless possibility of 'sides' developing in the congregation. Conflict stops the church from growing, as newcomers can become disillusioned that this church is jut like any other organization outside, and they expected it to be better.

Burnout is well catalogued in the church – many clergy suffer from it and need to take early retirement as a result. This is expensive for the church institution and tough on parishes, who may have their vicar off sick, or working part time, for a long period. Burnout is well commented on by many books about clergy life. Only one of my interviewees could be said to have left parish ministry through burnout – he had a full breakdown, and now covers for clergy on a locum basis, earning most of his income through sensitive and caring funeral work.

Frustration would be a large factor for me; having done what I felt I could in one parish, was it time to relocate yet again, with the accompanying business and stress, just to repeat my standard tricks for another parish? And what about the talents and abilities that I have in training and teaching that I was being asked to use in churches, but were unable to fulfil because of the pressure of the day to day life in the parish? Ally those feelings with a slight sense of boredom – that interesting enough as individual people are, and continue to be, the actual task had stopped holding my attention. I wanted to exercise other gifts that I believe to be God given, within a wider context. Alongside this is the feeling that the faith that I now have has moved and changed, (as Fowler anticipates and describes), and feeling well out on the edge in terms of faith in the diocese where I found myself.

Anne Rice, the acclaimed writer, recently described how she 'came out' of the Catholic Church:

In the name of Christ, I quit being a Christian. Amen.[12]

I see her point. Growing faith beyond that commonly experienced in most churches is a common comment from my research. Indeed, one clergy person commented that he felt he'd stepped away from the dance .... that 'the adventure was over'.

'Faith becoming a constraint' was coined as a reason for leaving by one priest who I spoke with, still within ministry and very well respected. He was alluding to the frequent gap between what clergy believe within their hearts and what clergy preach week by week. If you take Fowler seriously, how you preach to one congregation can become problematic, as you cherish those who are young in faith, challenge those who need to move on from that early stage, hold those undergoing transition and then meet the needs of the few who have arrived towards then end of the journey! Every diocese tends towards its own particular churchmanship in the majority, and so we can all become quite defensive, and not rocking the boat may be the safest option. How long you can commit to that particular compromise varies from person to person.

One area not cited in *Pastors in Transition* is the situation that gay clergy, male or female, find themselves in. The public stance of the institution, that practising gay relationships are not in keeping with the office, is profoundly painful. For many, their experience of this attitude has grown more hard line since they were ordained, and it now has a high profile and is the source of major disputes within the Church. One man pointed out to me that on most application forms for clergy posts, you can be 'married, single, divorced or widowed'. There is no tick box for 'civil partnership'. Ironically, most gay parish priests have no problem with members of the congregation, although older single men sometimes have problems gaining a first post, especially within the evangelical wing of the church, due to assumptions being made about their sexuality. Promotion is held to be less likely for gay men and women, so they may pursue other routes, often working instead within the confines of a cathedral close, where the dean holds sway, or as hospital or prison chaplains. Both these latter posts are outside of the usual diocesan constraints.

The other reason I would like to mention as a 'what can go wrong' is the mistaken vocation. Theoretically, this will happen less and less with improved selection procedures, but one man I talked with said that, after many years in office, he realized that it was never his vocation – it was his fathers'. Two broken marriages later, this man is comfortable with himself and working outside of the parish in a meaningful and creative way. Vocation can run down through families – it seems as though many clergy children may become out-and-out atheists or get ordained! Some are in the middle, but many clergy are children of the vicarage, and sometimes it seems as if they did it because they couldn't handle life outside of the security of the institution. The 'norm' of the vicarage life is atypical of normality outside of the vicarage. If you are used to relating in brief snippets, and being on call 24 hours a day, then the outside world could seem challenging, much as life outside the forces is a hard transition for many young serving 'squaddies'. So it may not be a vocation to the vicarage, but an inability to manage life outside of it that prompts some people towards ordination.

More details of what went wrong is the subject of a later chapter. For many serving as vicars, the ongoing pressure allied with the difficulties of the post that are inherent, are proving to be just about all that they can cope with. Not knowing how to get real support, and not being able to use that support, just makes the feeling of helplessness, that leads to stress and clergy burnout almost inevitable. I can hear archdeacons and bishops crying out that these are the people who never ask for help: but it is always the people who need the most help who find themselves unable to ask.

CHAPTER 6

Career structures in the Church

I remember being asked by one of the senior clergy at an early post-ordination session which of the group would like to be a bishop. There were 12 of us – nine men and three women. One man put up his hand, and we all nodded sagely. Yes, that made sense. He was more high church, had trained at Oxford, and yes, we could see this man becoming a bishop. He isn't yet, although a friend from my youth club days is, and I can see exactly why – I bet he's very, very good. Also, he's more evangelical, and the Church has swung that way over my years in ministry. But acknowledging the desire to be a bishop isn't common among clergy. We're probably thanking God that we don't have to face the task!

Curates, just beginning their life as ordained ministers, aren't usually looking that far ahead. Life is so different from before they turned their collars round. There are so many stresses and strains of this long period of what is essentially transition, that looking beyond next Sunday's sermon may be all that curates want to do. In the long term, once they've done a couple of years, the eyes reach above the parapet, and they search the 'situations vacant' in the *Church Times* and *Church of England newspaper*[1] for the promised land of their first incumbency. No matter how tough the curacy may have been, the problems may well be written off as 'someone else was in charge: things will be different once I have my own place ...'

And, to some extent, when you are an incumbent, how you manage the parish is up to you. But it's never as easy as you would like it to be – every parish has the person who has the hassock obsession or its equivalent. Churches collect such people and so they should, as churches are supposed to offer love to everyone, hassock obsession or not. The high motivation of being called by God to minister to God's people underlies all ministry, but after a while, the shine may start to tarnish:

> Many clergy ... do not have an overt ambition to high office, but are motivated by ideals of service. But many are hit mid-life by the realisation that there will just be 'more of the same' until retirement.[2]

There are 44 diocesan bishops in the Church of England and 70 suffragan bishops. Most diocesans were suffragan (second in the pecking order to the diocesan, usually one of two per diocese) prior to becoming a diocesan: it's a sort of bishop curacy, for lack of another way of explaining their role, but still senior to archdeacons, of whom there are around 116. In 2010 there are approximately 8,150 stipendiary clergy in the church, of whom about 1,650[3] are women. While non-stipendiary clergy may be area or rural deans, bishops are always stipendiary, as are archdeacons. So it's easy to see how hard it is to actually get 'promoted'. The actual expression is 'preferred'. That says it all, really. Just as with the proverbial curate's egg, some clergy are better than others. Once someone has been ordained, it is very difficult to suggest that maybe this was not a good idea for them, that maybe they should return to the lay life and pursue a previous career.

> However good the selection procedures are, there may be candidates whose difficulties or unsuitability only show up as training develops ... tutors find it difficult to get

any real doubts about suitability for ordination heard and addressed.[4]

Only one of the people that I contacted had been ordained and then not been offered another job post curacy. Questions were raised during training, but it was only as he came towards the end of his curacy that someone politely expressed doubts in his vocation. I can't imagine how hard that was for either of them. The counselling that now takes place at college level may sort out this terrible quandary before it arrives. My last curate knew of several people who left ministry during the first year after ordination; I do not know the details, but the upheaval and personal costs must have been enormous for both the individuals and their families, and for their incumbents and parishes as well as the diocesan officials who will all have worked to enable the curacy to happen.

We all know clergy who are worn out and need a break. Sadly, they don't always have the self-knowledge to do anything themselves, and the 'vicarage trap' means many cannot move on to another line of working:

> Ultimately it would have to be something 'fairly disastrous' to motivate them to go through 'all that it means to leave', so 'effectively you're trapped'. The couples spoke of having no other house to go to. Some had no other professional training or knew their previous skills were outdated, so there would be no alternative job.[5]

Indeed, a clergy friend who talked about flourishing in the post turned the whole interview on its head when he ended by saying: 'It's like the mafia – they've got your picture. We haven't got a house – so I'm stuck.' That vicarage, part of the stipend package, and the tie of tied housing is what keeps many clergy in the vicarage, when they really feel the need for a change of direction. But for many, especially those who were ordained relatively young, the tied house is exactly that.

The first incumbency is a steep learning curve. How to chair meetings, how to deal with the people at the door, how to relate to people who are talking about your predecessor, whom you may have never met, managing expectations, hopes and dreams. And, inevitably, managing the disappointment when it turns out that you too have feet of clay:

> Clergy need a good repertoire of spiritual and psychological strategies for coping with disappointment, discouragement, failure, opposition, depression, anxiety, fatigue and flattery.[6]
>
> Judicatory officers agree that today laypeople have higher expectations for their pastors ... Today laity are more knowledgeable and more willing to be vocal about concerns and issues ... The 'me generation' and the self-centredness, the 'I need to be pleased', and the pastors are pushed and pulled eighteen ways till Sunday. That stresses them.[7]
>
> Many ministers feel that they need to be perfect. Congregations generally expect that they should! ...
>
> Perhaps the greatest source of clergy stress comes from this sense of having to live with a mask, a 'pulpit persona'. The gradual erosion of the freedom to be one's authentic, true self, in favour of a religious performance, undermines the very springs of spiritual and psychological well-being. No wonder church leaders can become difficult people.[8]

These quotations show the variety of stressors that accompany the incumbent throughout their life, for it is very hard to stop being 'the vicar/rector'. Living in the vicarage means that to really get time out, you will have to travel out of the parish. In my last parish that usually meant walking to the station, meeting people as I walked. And because it was a small place, everyone knew I was the vicar, even when there was no dog collar being worn.

So the first incumbency is a time of rapid learning, more accommodating, and as Savage and Boyd-Macmillan indicate, slowly clergy can lose their authentic selves in the role that is expected of them. Attending training can actually make this worse; throughout my ministry, being part of a minority (woman, Emotion spiritual style, extrovert) meant that I often accommodated my natural instincts to become less conspicuous, quieter, less impulsive. I'm sure the others didn't realize that I was holding back! But that feeling of 'not belonging' is difficult to manage when it's nearly always there when you meet with colleagues. Perhaps the most obvious consequence of my discomfort was my inability to stick it out through any diocesan conference – I'd return home always at least 24 hours before they ended to recover. Others would say what a great conference and I'd wonder how it was possible for two people's perceptions to be so at odds. With increasing self-knowledge, I came to understand. But, as Savage and Boyd-Macmillan say, clergy can become very strange people.

There comes the point where most incumbents realize it's time to move to incumbency number two. It may be that they recognize that the parish needs someone with a different skill set, or just a different preaching style. That they need new challenges perhaps, or that the archdeacon has rung them and talked about a vacant parish 'that you'd be just right for'. So, after quite a period of soul searching, interviews, meeting the people and viewing vicarages, the minister moves, along with any family they have living with them.

According to the New Testament, all Christians are equal before God, but there is no doubt that some 'livings' or parishes, are more desirable than others, either in terms of how easy it is to be there, or that in some way this parish has clout.[9] It may be big, it may have a huge staff, it may be a 'Crown living'. At the moment, London is popular with clergy, but rural areas are not. Read the adverts, they tell you everything. So, if they are not one of the new older first incumbents, it is expected that clergy move from a parish where they cut their teeth as an incumbent on to a more complicated place. Once there, the minister repeats what worked at the previous place, and leaves out the mistakes. Life goes on. However:

> People enter Christian ministry with high hopes. It is not unusual for the ensuing struggle to erode personal resources and impassioned vision within the first five to ten years … the results of ministry are hard to measure, hard to pin down.[10]

Dissatisfaction may begin, possibly due to the amount of time that the minister can no longer spend with their family. People used to ask me what I was doing for Christmas as I said 'good-bye' after December services. When I replied 'I'm working' they looked non-plussed. 'Oh, of course' they'd reply. But that working meant that sometimes, I wasn't able to join in with events that took place when I was expected to be in church. That is the cost of ministry. You know about it before you begin, but the reality can be difficult at times:

> I think it's quite possible to refer to the parish as 'the other woman'.[11]

My family were always fantastically supportive of me, but the effect of ministry took its toll on them too. This was underlined for me on my first Easter out of the parish when my daughter simply said that she hadn't realized how much I'd worked over Easter until I was there this year. She wasn't being critical, simply commenting on the way that we'd lived for years. When the children were small, my husband took them to Legoland every Good Friday, so that I could kilter from event to event more easily. The number of clergy marriages that fail indicates how hard the life in the vicarage can be for the family of ministers.

The second and subsequent parishes are often longer stays than the first as children grow older and the family settles into the area. However, moving is a stressful business, finding a parish is hard and, as you get older, if the call to higher places doesn't come, life grows harder for many:

> The mid 50s are a difficult age for incumbents ... At this age they may feel that they have been passed over by the hierarchy ... 'I don't feel my gifts have been appreciated in the wider Church.'. He was voicing an oft-expressed view of disaffection ... this can lead to many older clergy experiencing weariness within a job they may have been doing for years.[12]

Men are also keener to be noticed than women according to Warren:

> The whole area of authority did not appear to be of primary interest to female clergy ... The concept of hierarchy, and who has authority over whom, though seen as important, appears to have less impact on female clergy than on male clergy.[13]

And I'm told that fewer women apply to be archdeacons, although many could, and many turn down the opportunity to be rural/area deans, the first step on the 'promotion' ladder.

For many years, it was very hard for women to be taken seriously as potential vicars. In the later 1990s, when I was looking for my second incumbency, several parishes implied that they weren't ready for a woman vicar yet – maybe next time. I understand that it is now easier, that along with *The Vicar of Dibley*, most people now recognize that women can indeed manage the job, and even do it well ... although there are still some 'no-go' areas for women, and these will remain for the foreseeable future. However, Wright reflects;

> One of the main reasons why some women have found the role of incumbent such a demanding one has not been through a lack of ability or good leadership qualities but because so many lay members of their church have been used to a more hierarchical structure of working.[14]

This was certainly my experience. Re-educating the congregation to take their part is hard work and takes years and the understanding of who makes a good leader. How women bishops work has yet to be discovered in this country.

Ironically, the lack of promotion opportunities seems to hit men far more than women, for although all the women in ministry that I know want women to be able to be bishops, no-one has confessed to having that ambition themselves, although I know several who would be brilliant in the role. Whether this seeming need to be noticed comes down to the traditional role of the man as breadwinner, who is seen for who he is through his work, where women seem to hang more loose to that is open to question. But lack of progress within the church is a real problem for many of the men that I work alongside.

The extra interest element for many who remain in the parish is to sit on diocesan committees. These are numerous in every diocese, relying on volunteers to work alongside clergy who administer all sorts of areas of church life – property, finance, children, youth, synod – and for many this may be where they find value. Attending meetings outside of the parish, being a voice that affects how things are done, can be a very satisfying thing for clergy. There needs to be a balance though, or the congregation will start to notice that the incumbent is off working for the diocese again, and once again, stress levels can rise.

Other clergy with a particular gift or talent may work in a paid capacity for a diocese or the central church. Every diocese has a string of officers who train clergy and lay people and run education departments and communications. Bishops need chaplains and some of the people with whom I spoke are now in these roles. Others move into cathedrals and work as residentiary canons, whose roles vary from cathedral to cathedral, and may move up that pecking order to be the dean, running their own cathedral – a high profile and taxing position. Still others may move into education, being a school chaplain or combining that with a parish part time. There are endless varieties of paid positions that can be found where a minister can exercise their ministry in a meaningful way, according to their talents. But they are few on the ground – of the 8,150 stipendiary ministers, the vast majority are parish priests, and the Church of England would collapse without them:

> The question must be whether, in the direction in which the Church is moving, it will have room for those gifted

creatively, as opposed to good at organisation, and whether it will not miss a great deal if it loses them, men and women, who have a vision of life that goes beyond efficiency, targets and goals.[15]

The problem is that the stress of being a parish priest is increasing, and so people are slowly but surely dropping out, and moving into other areas of work which are, according to my (very limited) research, more rewarding in terms of personal satisfaction, less stressful and ways of living out a vocation to priesthood in a more truthful way for those people. They also allow for a fuller use of the creativity that many clergy have but find can use less and less in the parish. Thus they side step any 'promotion' and find satisfaction outside of the role for which they seem to have been trained.

There are many fantastically talented and hard working parish priests, but the level of job satisfaction is low, and the Church needs to look at new ways of valuing and maintaining the priests who are the front line of the Church in the community.

CHAPTER 7

Listening to those who have left the parish

When researching this book, I began with people that I knew who had left parish ministry, or those to whom others led me. So there are undoubtedly large holes in the thoroughness of the research. The people that I talked to gave me time and energy, some telling their story for the first time, and I am enormously indebted to them all. This is far from the definitive answer to why clergy come out of parish ministry, just a stab at it.

The archdeacon's and bishop's views
I began by asking five archdeacons and a suffragan bishop, all on different occasions, why they thought people left parish ministry. The list given to me includes the following examples.

Loneliness, especially for single clergy

> The work of the priest is a lonely occupation.[1]
> For the single priest, the need and loneliness of close friendships was examined. For many, the loneliness of living alone in a community where so many expectations were laid upon them meant that their emotional, sexual and intellectual needs were often sublimated in the work.[2]

An inability to tell anyone what may be happening (including your partner) can make the minister shut down in some areas of communication. Some of the information and confidences that clergy live with can become a heavy burden. Being 'the vicar' also affects friendships within the parish – real friends, the ones you can be totally honest with, are few – and friends outside the parish may feel out of touch, as you have little time to give to them. It is a lonely role, and that's not often acknowledged.

Working on Sundays

Yes, we all know Sunday is the only day that clergy work ... ho ho. Not being able to take off for the weekend as most people do has a huge impact on life. One of the biggest changes in my life since coming out of the parish is the ability to do what I want to most Sundays, even if that's just lying in bed reading the newspaper for an extra hour. And the chance to miss church if I want to.

The working hours, and the criticism if you are not seen to be working 'all the hours that God sends'

I wore my dogcollar to the supermarket, and chatted to people as I went round to keep the guilt at bay if I was there on a 'working day'. How mad is that, when the working hours were usually from getting up until I went to bed? Some people demand a justification of the minister's life that can feel intrusive and ultimately prove to be destructive.

Following a successful priest

I remember telling a curate once that following a poor parish priest is the best way to be thought of as a real star. But if you come after a good one – you are always being told how that person used to do it better. People don't realize just how hurtful that is.

Handling expectation

We have already dealt with this, but it continues to be a very difficult area for many clergy. Wright picks up on a common finding among women clergy:

> One of the main reasons why some women have found the role of incumbent such a demanding one has not been through a lack of ability or good leadership qualities but because so many lay members of their church have been used to a more hierarchical structure of working.[3]

Expectation of how clergy work is based upon male working patterns. A woman incumbent often works differently from the men that she follows – and there may be problems as the parish get used to a different form of leadership. Quite apart from the tendency from some (largely older men in my experience) to tell 'the little woman' how to do the job.

Having a non-stipendiary minister on the staff

While many NSMs are excellent, others can be a bit of a 'curate's egg' – good in parts. And even the ones who are brilliant at the ministry can be eroding when they tell you how it's always been done here – because they may have been in this parish for the whole of their lives. And, in my experience, little is taught stipendiary clergy about the management of volunteer priests. So they are both a blessing, and a possible curse.

The other 'problem' for the vicar, who has to be in church for 47 weeks of the year, is that NSMs can turn down doing something if it's not convenient, and therefore be seen to cherry pick their ministry. And why not – they are volunteers after all! But on a tough day, NSMs can sometimes inadvertently rub salt into the wound. I spoke with one NSM, Joan, who was just moving parishes at the time. She had just covered a period of illness in the parish, despite being clear that her vocation was not to regular parish ministry. She doubted whether the powers that be ever considered what her vocation might be other than parish-based ministry. She is called to work among people, to love them and get to know them better where they are. She suggested that maybe closing some old buildings would free up clergy to do their work more efficiently and more easily. She is at present chaplain at the local civic offices and has no agenda there. This ministry is beginning to flourish, quietly. She feels that non-stipendiary ministry is 'really important' as it gives the church ministers who can be more creative in what they do, but that the church saw them as propping up the system. She questioned whether the church asks too much when placing NSMs with parish clergy – she said they can be empowering, but they can also be toxic. This can lead to resentment, as NSMs can cherry pick! Ideally the ministers should empower each other, but this only comes through a sacrificial relationship.

Boundaries – both on the part of ministers and the congregation

One archdeacon told a story that a curate was at home on his day off when a member of the congregation knocked on the door. He was in his underwear, so he didn't answer. He then found the lady looking in at him through his kitchen window as he ate breakfast – in his boxer shorts.

Alternatively, a colleague often has a late breakfast on his day off in his dressing gown, and if one of the congregation comes round, his wife shows them in!

No end points

Clergy rarely tick off a piece of work as a job well done – most of it lingers and will never finish. Even funerals need follow up, if time allows. And the job is getting bigger and bigger:

> The disconnect between what clergy are expected to do, to achieve ('Be a fresh expression! Keep paying the quota! Both! And!) and the means by which clergy are expected to achieve all this (sustaining the pattern of Herbertism), is getting bigger and bigger. It is impossible. So they leave.[4]

A letter to the *Church Times* of 30 July 2010 expressed concern that clergy are having to take time off sick, suffering from stress – and they have benefices (collections of small parishes under one minister, usually with the assistance of lay ministers and NSMs) comprising between 11 and 15 churches. It concludes:

> Given current budgetary constraints affecting dioceses, and another swath of reorganisation being implemented across the Church of England, is it not now time for national guidelines to be drawn up to help dioceses in developing realistic job-descriptions, including limiting the number of parishes any one incumbent can reasonably be expected to serve?[5]

Did I leave for this reason? It contributed. When I moved from St Somewhere else, where I found two churches more than I could manage, the first priority was one church building, no more. This was emphasized by a recent vacancy advertised in the *Church Times*:

> We want you to be freed for real ministry! ... House for Duty priest ... to care for five small and friendly villages.[6]

The advertisement went on to stress that they were going to look after the buildings, so that 'for 2½ days you can ...'. It sounded pretty full on to me – but fascinating that the buildings weren't part of the brief. There is a recognition that if the person was to be effective in 2½ days, something had to go from the usual duty round. Perhaps this will catch on, and more clergy will be freed from the care of (often listed) buildings, for which few of us had any training. However, at the time of writing the post is still vacant.

Clergy identity merging with the role

> A combination of subconscious processes and an internally imposed, but never conclusively defined conformity, leads to the clergy always being on best behaviour, and ultimately to an 'erosion of the freedom to be the authentic self' ... This is the Litany of the Cult of Nice.[7]

When my father came to hear me preach for the first time, he commented I was 'very good. You just haven't quite got the manner yet.' I decided that the day I did get the manner was the day that I quit parish ministry. I like to think that I never did 'get the manner'. A friend once joked that a local Anglo Catholic priest even wore black pants and pyjamas. I don't know if that was literally true, but you get the meaning.

This merging leads to personal hurt when the vicar is criticized; it also means that clergy personality vanishes under the persona of the kind, nice vicar. Role confusion means that you become defensive and can become overactive to compensate for that defensiveness. It is enormously pervasive, and clergy can feel that their personality is slowly but surely ebbing away. No wonder they sometimes break out in a spectacular manner.

When I was being interviewed for posts outside of parish ministry, the 'celebrity' factor was always asked: how will you cope when you stop being someone that everyone knows? I always said that I would love to be anonymous again. They didn't always believe me, but I was right. I love being me again, not the vicar.

Personal charisma can be 'sucked out' of ministers through
overexposure to synodical government and administrative tasks
That creative clergy may be squeezed out of the church has been mentioned; such clergy may find the Synodical process does not play to their natural talents and Morley alluded to the possibility that clergy of a more creative nature will find themselves being squeezed out of the Church.[8] Clergy are expected to take part in synods, and the charismatic people are often encouraged to stand for General Synod. The question of whether they have the right personality type for handling that committee work is rarely asked: Bishop Brian Castle recently wrote about his first experience of General Synod 'as I was losing the will to live ...'.[9] Clergy do get noticed at General Synod, and this can be the way of preferment, but is this helpful if it involves that person being bored past their ability to cope? I sat on Diocesan Synod for 18 months before I found the effect it was having on me so awful that I stood down: I left each meeting feeling as if I had been hit on the head by a hammer – totally brain dead.

I know that some colleagues expected me to apply for 'preferment' as an archdeacon at one point. The fact that this would not have been a good job for me, because of who I am, made no sense to them – surely a good parish priest would also make a good archdeacon? My knowledge of my personality and how I function says 'no' very loudly. I could not have managed the committee meetings, the tough management decisions and living with the sometimes painful consequences. Tough decisions need to be made in the church, but I wasn't the person to do that as my main activity. I am quite capable of such decision making, but I do not flourish in such a role, and never will.

The administrative side of the post can be enormous, and as some of it is legal work (especially weddings) it can take a lot of time. Some parishes have clerks who fill in the books and forms, but if you work in a parish without such people, the ongoing administration can be overpowering. As fewer parishioners can manage the parish accounts as they grow more complex, so clergy also have to become book keepers. Without a secretary, many clergy produce services week by week, or produce notice sheets. This is all work that in some parishes is undertaken by paid or voluntary help, but in others, the task falls to the parish priest.

Working on the 'important and urgent' through to 'not important and not urgent' criteria, I used to have a pile of papers that were to be looked at 'when I had a minute'. These were the unimportant and not urgent pieces of information, often courses available etc. Every 3 months I put them straight in the recycling – they were all out of date.

The consequences of these stressors are seen from time to time:

> The likely effects of these hidden conflicts in ministry would be illness, alcohol or other drug dependence, and emotional and marital breakdown.[10]

These are the effects that the archdeacons were well aware of, and saw in their clergy all too frequently. The cost of early retirement is high, to the individual churches who may feel that they have somehow 'failed' their minister, to the Church, paying pensions, and to the individuals concerned, whose families also pay the price.

All of the books that I reference talk about clergy breakdown. It is far more common than widely realized, and worryingly difficult to address.[11]

Personal experiences

Some people who have made the break.[12] All names have been changed to protect the identity of the people who spoke to me.

Diocesan employees

These people are all ordained, have worked in the parish and now work as a diocesan member of staff, usually in the role of training lay or ordained people.

Antony undertook special training to move from the parish in Change skills and strategies. He went part time in the parish while studying, and paid for the course himself. He set up in consultancy until the right diocesan post came along and he applied successfully. He questions why the training budget for clergy is not all used up every year – why don't clergy want to get themselves better equipped for their work? He believes that a lot of clergy pressure comes from them not thinking through their priorities. Antony does a lot of work with clergy teaching them how to be active learners, helping them to reframe in usable ways. He comments that clergy groups tend to be hierarchical and competitive. If you can change that environment, you increase learning.

Alex's wife was ordained a few years after he was. He began ministry in the parish, studying for a PhD at the same time. Once his wife was ordained, he applied for a diocesan post simply to ensure that they had time for the family. The specialist knowledge and expertise that he has means he has held a senior posts for many years.

Other people that I spoke to clearly saw their diocesan post as the next stage in their ministry. They are able to use specific talents and abilities, and feel as if they are genuinely contributing to the life of the Church. The number of posts within diocesan structures is decreasing though, as dioceses have less and less money to utilize, so these people are also suffering from work piling up around them, with no end in sight.

A few people go to work for the Church's central office, perhaps as a selector for ordination candidates, or as a specialist such as the national children's officer. Again, these people see themselves as having particular skills that the whole church can access through their work. Many help out in local parishes on Sundays. For clergy couples, this can provide a good balance for one of the partners.

Chaplains

Becoming a school, prison or hospital chaplain may be a tough form of ministry, but you are employed by another agency than the Church of England, so appraisal and ongoing training are the norm. Chaplains also have set hours, so work–life balance may be easier to achieve. Neither do they live 'on the job', so boundaries are set.

Sally is a church school chaplain. She works school hours, and school terms, so she is free to be home for her children around school hours. Her husband is also ordained, so this is a good solution to parenting and family life issues that can arise when both parents are in parish ministry. She likes working as part of a larger group of people, finding the isolation of parish ministry unhelpful. As a trained teacher, the school environment was welcoming, and she brings her previous experience into her new role. She had found parish life difficult at times – she felt unsupported and isolated. There was enormous pressure to work 'into the ground' and the pressure on the family life became extreme. She doesn't work from home now, and pastoral need is presented literally, right in front of her in school. Her boundaries are firmly in place – she lives quite a distance from the school, so there are no parishioners appearing on the doorstep just when you don't want to see them. Her comments about her training included:

- The college was running on a more monastic model than was helpful for her (she travelled into college from a distance away).
- The college felt more male/resident family focussed.
- She would have preferred a more apprenticeship type of training.

Sue is a hospital chaplain, working part time. After training at a theological college, she wasn't able to find a curacy that was appropriate – her husband's work is based in a major city. A friend offered her a non-stipendiary curacy, which she accepted. They then moved south to cut commuting time, and she had another child. After a couple of years, she was offered the post as associate priest at their parish church, which she accepted, and had some good years there. Moving on to become vicar elsewhere, she discovered that what parishes say they want is not always what they mean;

> Where clergy from one churchmanship struggle in a church with a very different churchmanship, they often feel unaffirmed and rejected. If they see themselves as representatives of God in a congregation that has little liturgical appreciation and wants a preaching vicar, the internal struggle will affect them at a psychic level.[13]

Sue changed the liturgy, and worked very hard. Her problems soon became apparent when the people who put most money in the collection objected to the changes. She found herself being pressed by the diocese for their money, and the parish which really hadn't decided how much they wanted liturgical change. This had been the face of a power struggle, which she recognised she couldn't 'win'. She resigned after a year, and now works in chaplaincy.

Cathedral canons work for their dean, as part of a cathedral chapter. Charles is canon chancellor at a Midlands cathedral. He had only recently arrived when I spoke to him. I hadn't seen Charles since theological college, where he and I were good friends. He was one of the youngest men there, and I remembered him as very bright and lots of fun. As an 'out' gay minister, he knew that it would be hard to get a post such as archdeacon (looking back to the furore over Jeffrey John). So he applied for a cathedral post, where personal sexuality is not likely to be an issue.

Charles also used the word 'flourish' – he needed to be in a place where he had a wider vision of the church, and a cathedral gives that breadth. His perception of the church was that 'bright' people are given either diocesan officer type posts, or more demanding parish posts. However, he commented that many posts are more demanding than it might appear and it would be very helpful if the church recognized this, rather than just automatically giving higher prestige to the diocesan posts. He commented that we only have one life, and his relationship with his partner is more important than the church (they are civil partners). He spoke to the dean about his sexuality before applying for this post, and the dean replied that it wasn't a determining factor.

Charles clearly loves his post, but voiced several important factors about life in the Church for civil partners and he has been with his partner for a very long time. These included:

- Issues about pension rights. They have only been in a legal relationship for a short while, but their personal relationship has outlived many marriages. This issue is still on the agenda at General Synod.

- How does the Church deal with those in civil partnerships? Charles is not defined by his status, but there are issues around role that need to be clarified.

Charles feels that his vocation should be about liberation – how to be in the Church, and not be oppressive, or oppressed, by the institution. He likes living a few miles away from the office – helps boundaries no end! Any role confusion that he had as vicar have been left behind. He feels things will get worse for gay clergy before they get better. There is a need for greater awareness and professionalism. The Church is now a global church, and we can't do theology as we used to, and we clearly can't go back, yet the new way forward has not yet emerged. Charles also noted his bishop is a workaholic: I think many of us would use that word for our bishops, who don't always model good patterns of ministry and boundaries to their clergy, yet are inundated by their 'in-tray' when they look at the desk.

Along with gay issues, Charles is very aware of issues of race, which the Church is only slowly working through. When asked about the experience of gay clergy, Charles said he felt more and more go into chaplaincy or cathedrals, as life in ministry is easier within those contexts than in the parish – not because of parishioners, but because of the attitudes of some bishops and of the Church as an institution.

During my work I came across a whole group of people whom I hadn't originally considered; women who have young children and husbands who cannot pick up much of the childcare because they work long and demanding hours out of the home.[14]

> Past research has shown that women ministers tend to leave ministry more than their male counterparts do ... the women are less likely to be chosen as senior pastors in flourishing and desirable churches ... some women leave active ministry to care for family and children, at least for a number of years. Men seldom do this. Men ministers tend to be more career-driven than women and less likely to drop out of active ministry for any period of time.[15]
>
> They said that they had had problems creating a private life apart from their ministerial role and many often felt that their work did not give them enough time for their children.[16]

Dot works in the London diocese, as a 'house for duty' priest, part time. Thus, in exchange for living in a vicarage at little expense, she covers the Sunday duties and 2 days a week in the parish. Her husband works full time and she has two small children. This is working well for them as a family. She described her college as 'clueless' regarding exercising ministry outside of a parish or academic context, and said that she wished she'd opted for a course rather than a college for her training, feeling that would have equipped her better for the role she now occupies.

Daisy is married to a parish priest, and is described as the 'associate priest' in the parish. She is unpaid, but does paid work for 1 day a week within the chapter, encouraging vocations – an area where she has always been active. She is not happy with this arrangement, but neither Daisy nor her husband can find something more extensive for her to do. They have a toddler and neither of them would want her to be working full time, there's just a sense of frustration that after the training and commitment there is nothing more productive and fulfilling.[17] She said it's hard to be creative in finding other ways to be a priest. Her experience of training was mixed. She attended college, and really enjoyed the community aspect but found the experience very de-skilling.

Elaine, a daughter of the vicarage, lives in London, and has a variety of jobs that she does, few of which pay very much. After training on a course, she worked at a central London church over the period that she had two children, and then decided that parenting small children when your husband also works long hours is not very compatible with parish ministry. She left full-time stipendiary ministry and now has a portfolio of ministerial work. She is a published writer and speaker on *Thought for the Day*. She agrees that what she does is 'all good stuff, but there's too much of it'. She believes the central issue for many women who have young children is the inordinate amount of time taken up by ministry – including the stuff that continues in your head after you turn the computer off. She enjoys being a priest at the school gate, and spending time with her three children. She commented that the area of London where she works is quite 'male and clubby'. This is an observation that many women in ministry have made, and that the men find it hard to recognize. While women can cope with this aspect of ministry, it is tough for the first women who enter that club.

Elaine also recognizes that the Church takes for granted an enormous amount of financial support from partners whose support enables their spouses to minister, but who may not be Christians themselves:

> For many, the need to spend more time with family and children was not a motivation that stood alone; commonly

it was accompanied by other motives – exhaustion being a major one. In more than a quarter of the cases, respondents told us that they felt both overburdened by the demands of their parish and guilty over the resulting neglect of their families.[18]

So these creative and lateral-thinking women have carved out time for family by turning their backs on full-time parish life.

The National Association of Diocesan Advisors in Women's Ministry sees the way that women are deployed as slightly different from men; the numbers that are non-stipendiary/self-supporting are higher, and some of these women are found in a house for duty type role. Many work in a self-supporting role (see Appendix 2) where they live in a family home, and just claim expenses from the parish.

This is great for the parishes, and the wider Church, but, as with all 'house for duty', relies on the women having income apart from their ministry. This is a thorny issue, but all the women that I spoke to had partners who were effectively paying for their ministry, and could do so because they earned a good income. Thus these women are exercising a priestly minister within the parish, but on different terms from most of their male colleagues.

Clergy working outside recognized ministerial roles
This was my starting point for this book; there are no records of how many of us exist, but the conversations that I had with those who were living away from parish ministry, who really had leapt the vicarage wall, shed an interesting light of what ministry can be like.

Felix was a 'successful' priest, who probably would have become a bishop had he not left parish ministry. Felix trained many years ago at Cambridge and Oxford. His training for ordination raised serious questions that threatened his vocation and challenged his essential identity. Too much time was spent on his ecclesiological and theological formation and too little attention was given to reflection upon his life experiences and personal development. He marked time rather than grew as a human being. He spoke highly of several iconic figures, Archbishop Michael Ramsey, Gustavo Gutierrez and Bishop John Robinson, who had a profound influence upon his faith formation.

He had been ordained for 34 years and had served the institutional church in parish, sector (higher education) and cathedral ministry. During that time he had neglected his children, his marriage and himself, and frequently missed the signals that they were sending. His wife (his marriage survived) says she has rediscovered the man she fell in love with.

When Felix spoke to his dean about resigning, following a 3-month sabbatical, the dean was supportive and encouraging. The bishop was supportive but didn't know what to say. Felix continued that he struggled to stay connected to the world during his ministry. While he loved the Church, he had always had a greater love of the Kingdom. When the Church went through the Decade of Evangelism, writing endless mission statements, he became increasingly frustrated and detached from the Church as institution.

His last role was within a cathedral chapter. He now describes himself as a 'loose canon' and after taking early retirement has developed a portfolio ministry, offering and exercising his gifts on his terms. He said that he had 'rediscovered' his vocation after leaving the stipendiary ministry. It felt as if he'd been released from prison and had thrown off the shackles that had entrapped him: emotive expressions, which he expanded. His ministry was marked throughout by an inner loneliness, but he found his cell group from college days had been a great support. He added that he had come to the awful discovery that 'the Church was often the place of rebellion against God, a skulking in the bushes from his presence'.

Felix is happy to call himself a Christian and Anglican. He uses a verse from Psalm 31 as his mantra: 'You have set my feet in a large room'. His frustration with the Church is that he thinks it always tends towards a safe and narrow vision of God. His time in Latin America many years ago is not only fundamental to who he is and what he believes, but also enlarged his understanding of the Christian gospel and the Kingdom. What had facilitated his early retirement was the fact that he had his own house where he could live and the support of his wife's income. He knew he had marketable skills, and networked openings in this country and in the USA. He now manages his time more successfully for himself, his family and his friends. A genuine sense of fulfilment and happiness has replaced the inner loneliness and frustrations of the past. He offers spiritual direction. He preaches widely and assists regularly in parish and sector ministry and has made excellent use of his skills as a communicator and teacher. The process of leaping the wall had been amazingly liberating. He no longer has any regrets about his decision to take early retirement.

Resigning was a tough decision, with lots of 'what if?' questions. Felix still questions how good the Church is as an institution at developing and cherishing the skills of its professional ordained staff and handling the expectations that are placed upon its ministers. Is being fulfilled in ministry always looking for 'the next big job'? He concluded this very honest conversation by saying that he now had an enormous sense of relief and had come alive again.

Francis was ordained 25 years ago, and was non-stipendiary for many years. He trained at a college part time, while maintaining his teaching job during the day. When he was asked to be redeployed as a teacher, he decided to enter stipendiary ministry. He had a successful curacy, but after 6 months as vicar in a different diocese he suffered a complete breakdown. He was helped by a specialist counsellor at the time, but in the end needed time in hospital. The bishop at the time was not helpful and his relationship with his wife broke down. He took early retirement and for 5 years had no ministry at all. Francis's wife divorced him and he felt very alone and unsupported during this period.

After this time, a local vicar offered Francis limited ministry at the church where he had been worshipping since his breakdown. This was the beginning of Francis' real recovery, leading to an agreement to work a set number of hours in the parish, supervised by the vicar. When this excellent vicar moved on, Francis also relocated to assist at another church. He has now married again and works to support local clergy in their ministry, conducting many funerals and taking locum services for clergy on holiday or study leave.

How could life have been improved for Francis? While he was undergoing the breakdown, the diocese seemed unable to understand or hear his distress. After he retired, he felt completely abandoned. He still feels that the church is not making use of this experience of mental illness, and neither has he been recognized as healed. He feels that he has been restored to ministry, but that has not been acknowledged officially.

Felix and Francis both had their own property, as did I. Leaving the vicarage when you have no home to move into is a huge psychological barrier, but one that the next priest was able to scale.

George was the only single minister that I talked with. Leaving parish life was therefore extremely hard for him financially – he took what work he could (stacking shelves in a supermarket for several years) while working up a niche role as a journalist and therapist. George used the phrase 'the adventure was over' when I asked what had finally caused the move. He has been ordained for 27 years at the time of our conversation, all of those spent in London.

George trained at a college, and his curacy became particularly challenging when his incumbent died after just one year together. He was an elderly man who had been persuaded to take on one last role. George became minister-in-charge until a new vicar came. His parish ministry had been a good time, and he enjoyed being a priest, but after 20 years, and much to his surprise, he just knew that the next move would not be to another church. He had no idea of what he would do, and although the finances were very tough, he enjoyed the freedom that his resignation brought. He now works in counselling, using mindfulness, leads retreats, writes books and contributes to various national newspapers. He believes his present vocation is to face his own suffering and to be kind to people. A hermit by nature, he also enjoys the company of the world. His preferred form of worship is now pure silence with a candle. Words are not helpful.

George said that he isn't interested in labels; that God is in truth wherever it is found. He feels he hasn't let go of the adventure, just one form of it. He felt that his training catered for the immature, that there was no direct expression of truth, just ideas about truth. Concerning the age at which people train, George felt it was irrelevant: it's more to do with attitude. 'We don't grow wiser, we may even grow more stupid.' George feels that keeping an open mind is critical, but fewer people follow that in the Church today. George feels the Church has become more insecure and, as a result, more tribal.

James was an incumbent for many years, but when his marriage broke down he resigned from the parish and began working outside of ministry, eventually rising to a highly responsible position in local government. Over the course of many years, he slowly took on priestly duties, and became a non-stipendiary minister within a team. The subsequent break down of his second marriage meant he resigned this position and once again ceased ministry. James now carries a sense of shame and awareness of the damage that this has caused the churches that he has served in, and he remains a member of an active congregation in a lay capacity. He now mainly lives alone, and is enjoying the solitude.

James trained many years ago, but wonders whether he was originally ordained to gain his father's approval. I have known James for some years and know that his ministry was effective, but this is an area that Warren covers[19] – who are we being ordained for? How strongly our parents affect us as adults is being more understood as time goes by; many of us spend our lives seeking that approval, and ordination may be a good way to do that.

One of the people who I spoke to who is highly regarded as a training incumbent and is still in parish ministry said that he thought sometimes clergy have affairs because they feel so 'chained in' by parish life. If this is combined with dissatisfaction with their marriage, then disaster can follow. Bearing in mind the high level of clergy marriage stress due to the working conditions of ministers, it's surprising more clergy don't have to resign in the way that James did.

John was the first parish priest that I know who moved out of parish ministry, during the time he was my own vicar. After training and a curacy, he was a successful university chaplain, and moved on to be the vicar in the tough inner city area, where many of the students lived. He was a great vicar, and it was a bolt from the blue when he announced that he was going to be the director of the local voluntary sector 'umbrella' body

John and his family owned their own house because the diocese paid a housing allowance as there was no university chaplaincy house. So moving out of the vicarage was fairly easy for them. John believes that any vocation should involve choice which means that clergy ought to be able to do another job. He saw many clergy, some of whom had lost their enjoyment of the job, but moved from one parish to the next as it was the only pattern that they felt they could do. So John wanted to prove himself in secular employment as part of his vocation. Though he intended to, he never returned to parish ministry because several interesting secular jobs presented themselves. However he has always been licensed to a local parish and served on Bishop's Council for 5 years.

Talking with him after many years, we reflected on how intensive the ministry was in that place. Half of the vicarage had been turned into a Toc-H sponsored house, where young Christians lived as a community, as a way of committing to the people there. It was all very incarnational, and the presence of the people next door – five of whom have since been ordained – was a great support for the vicarage family. That, and the fact that many children regarded the vicarage garden as their local park, had stayed with me down through 20 years. I remembered his wife commenting on the vicarage there, that their 8-year-old son slept at the front of the house, and they would never hear if something was lobbed in from outside through his window as happened more than once in the room under his; most of the house was down a long hallway. It was a very tough area, and John and his family had entered into that community with heart and soul. However, they were frequently burgled, and several very difficult people lived close by. John was getting very tired after 5 years, and realized that he was approaching burnout.

Originally, working outside the parish was to be temporary, but John was good at it and felt fulfilled. After 10 good years working with the voluntary sector, he was offered secondment to the city council as it approached unitary government because he understood the city so well. This was also enjoyable and he felt that he was working for change for many deprived young people in the city. The onset of Parkinson's disease forced early retirement though he has many voluntary commitments including one Sunday a month at the parish where we knew him.

John is a wise man, and we reflected on the stress of ministry together. He was fortunate to have a group of people around him, both ordained and lay, who made the inner city parish work exciting though exhausting. Without this group, the work might have been impossible. So many city churches have concentrated on the those who attend (often not local residents) meaning that the church no longer exists for every one who lives in the parish; something that Grace Davie recognizes:

> What is relatively new is the introduction of the market principal into some parts of the Church of England. This is ... best illustrated by ... the flourishing churches of suburbia which attract large numbers of like-minded individuals from a relatively wide geographical area, well beyond the parochial boundaries. There are, very often, articulate individuals who choose – for doctrinal or aesthetic reasons – the type of church to which they want to belong.[20]

John discussed this theme – that the congregation have expectations of care to themselves, and find it hard to see beyond the church walls. In an inner city parish, there may be a need to 'import' some members of the congregation for a while – and John did this, but then the local people need to be taking over. But money is always short in such areas, and so the parishes can now come under threat. John's parish has now been joined with two other inner city parishes; however, the other two are far more middle class, and have eclectic congregations, as they are surrounded by the city shopping area, a situation that can be easily recognized:

> Clergy can be squeezed both by the wider diocesan systems, which increasingly look to parishes to contribute at least the cost of providing them with a priest; and by the PCC which is encouraged by such an approach to see the Vicar as 'theirs' – the one whom they have paid for and by extension whom they no employ.[21]

Difficult as it may be, John sees the only way forward as a return to loving the people of the area, of a church that is inclusive rather than exclusive, for example the lack of finance for parishes which can not support full-time clergy may mean that clergy need to find local employment while remaining the vicar and living in the vicarage.

Linda, who is single, and very good indeed at the work, described parish ministry as juggling 500 balls. There are too many bits and pieces, and at times she felt she was doing nothing really well. Linda's college experience was positive but she felt that other previous training had been more formational. While her curacy had prepared her quite well for her first incumbency, she would have valued more effective input in the early stages of her new role. At times, she struggled with loneliness and issues around the vicar not being a 'normal' person. Linda loves people and the local community, and in many ways feels fulfilled in her role. She added, however, that 'stuff' e.g. paperwork, was a drain on her time and energy, and she felt frustrated at its impact on her ability to engage more effectively with the gospel. Being a 'grassroots' person, she has no desire for further advancement within the Church. Linda is seeking ways of attaining a better work–life balance.

My final conversation was with an ordained clergywoman, Louise, whose husband Peter is the local vicar. She works for the church in a non-stipendiary role. The main area that we covered was to do with the Clergy Disciplinary Measure (CDM),[22] which had been used by some members of the church against her husband. This measure has been law since 2006. Four days after the act became part of canon law, her husband found that a measure had been taken out against him. He remained in post while this legal action took place, at great cost to his personal health, and that of his family. The person fronting the action had a personal grudge against Peter, and Louise described his actions as bullying. The diocesan bishop cannot support a vicar who has a CDM taken out against them, but Louise said the diocese, especially the suffragan bishop, were 'brilliant' in their support. They found themselves caught up in a judicial process that could have cost a lot of money, and she pointed out that there is no equivalent procedure that clergy can take out against the laity. A few years later, Peter has had a life-threatening illness and is now coping with the after effects. Louise added that having been through the CDM process once, she was not prepared to risk it again – it had been at huge cost, and most people leave a parish after the measure.

Their diocese is stretched to breaking point to the extent where she believes 15 per cent of the clergy are off sick with stress related illness. She believes the problems lie in the expectations of the laity, who have a plethora of ideas as to what the vicar should be doing. There is a huge emphasis on conservation, and she wants people to concentrate on what it means to be a Christian; it's like trying to turn a 'supertanker' around, and the task needs a huge amount of energy and enthusiasm. Locally the bishop is great for encouraging creative forms of ministry, but there's little money to back up the efforts made. Louise added that she believed that after about 15 years of ministry, people begin to leave. Clergy get tired of repeating the same things. She feels you have to have lots of internal strength if you are to 'rock the boat'. When I asked what she would like to do next, it was clear that she and Peter want to stay in some sort of ministry, but they're not sure they have the energy to continue in the parish setting at the moment.

A sample of clergy who are sticking

To provide a balance, this section provides a snapshot of three very different parish priests, who are finding fulfilment within their role and calling. All of them are known to me personally, and all are highly respected within their dioceses. Their church-manship is varied, as is their personal history.

Peter has been ordained for 25 years. He studied at a residential college, and has moved around the same diocese during his ministry. Known within that diocese as a 'safe pair of hands' he sometimes is the second port of call for curate where something has gone wrong in their first placing, and he takes over and works towards success with these individuals. He runs efficient churches, and has moved into parishes that are of high standing within the community. He enjoys talking, preaching, teaching and has moved towards a more liberal personal theology, and says that he feels people appreciate him. He finds his creative outlets outside of ministry, enjoying walking, photography and football. He and his wife have worked to keep their intimacy alive and well by taking a day off together mid week. His attitude towards Saturday is that he 'won't go looking for work' on that day, and does the minimum. Peter tends to write his sermons on Saturday morning, and then switch off. He has served time as an area/rural dean and enjoyed the pastoral side of that work, coming alongside other clergy. Peter was single for the first 10 years of his ministry and then married a widow, so inheriting a ready-made family. His widow was married to an Anglican vicar, so she had a full understanding of what life is like in a vicarage.

Peter said that he came out of college with the basics for ministry – visiting, preaching, getting to know people. College threw him in at the deep end sometimes, such as a placement which included psychiatric patients, but that the value of his residential experience may now be undervalued by others. His work includes training curates, and he reflected that the present formal CME/post-ordination training input is perhaps too academic, leading to dissatisfaction among the curates. He would rather see a more practical training take the place of what is often a Masters level degree course. Does this sow seeds of frustration perhaps?

Peter now feels called to help the Church to become a special community, kind and prayerful, with a sense of humour and minimal gossip. He closed by wondering if a lack of joy about being with people is undermining some ministries.

Sarah was a teacher for 20 years before training for ministry. She had a curacy within her home diocese and is now a well-respected vicar within that diocese. She also assists the training department and has a good track record as a clergy trainer, with both curates and further CME work.

Trained on the local course, which she felt was very good, her curacy caused great stress. She felt her maturity and experience were not taken into account. Her collaborative style caused problems, which were eased after a Myers–Briggs workshop enabled greater understanding of how the two personalities interacted. Her incumbency has been less stressful but she acknowledges that she is a workaholic. As her husband has similar working patterns, this does not cause problems for them.

She talked of problems among curates on CME, some caused by more extreme attitudes among the men who don't affirm women in ministry. This is clearly a subject for her regular supervision sessions with her curates, and she is disciplined in keeping up this supervisory role. Sarah questions the different forms of ministerial training now taking place, although she reflected that some people who are in ministry will not want to be incumbents, so a different style of training is appropriate. She is sometimes frustrated by an unwillingness to try all aspects of parish ministry, while enjoying the diversity of talent and ability that her various staff bring. Her team recently had a Myers–Briggs training day which was very good, and enabled reflection together about the make up of the team. Sarah finds some of her staff less collaborative, but she has a firm management style, but is always fair, and this engenders good working relationships.

Sarah has an unusual working pattern in that she tends not to take one day off in a week, but to take off longer lengths of time when she has enough in lieu. She is very flexible day by day, enjoying long lunches. She works to the Benedictine model of rest/play/work. She closed by echoing the words that I have heard repeated by many older, wiser clergy, that you need to be very secure in yourself if you are to remain in ministry.

Martin is my own parish priest. When we moved, I spent a few weeks wandering the local churches finding one where I felt 'at home'. I immediately felt welcomed by the 'regulars' at just the right level, and have remained. This church has one of the fastest growing congregations in the diocese. Most of these new Christians attend the second service of the day on Sunday, which has less structure and is far more informal than the earlier service – which has an older congregation with more traditional worship. The music at 10.30 is led by one of a selection of worship teams, and the youth and children's work is led by a trained group of people at the same time. Alpha is run regularly, and people find their way into the church by a variety of means. Perhaps the most obvious feature of the 10.30 congregation is that many have not come from a Christian background, and they are the younger families who are moving into the area: the town is at the end of the Thames Gateway development and is surrounded by new estates.

Martin has been the vicar here for 7 years, and is in his first incumbency. He finds support through various means; his wife, Fran, grew up in a vicarage, and is at present training for ministry herself. He has two prayer triplets, one outside the church, and the other of trusted people from the church. He has a mentor, who stretches and challenges him, as well as belonging to the New Wine network, and is the local co-ordinator.

Martin had a very distinct call to ordination, and sees himself as a vision holder, who releases people to work together to achieve the vision. He certainly manages to release people into various ministries, with a great ability to spot leaders, and then equip them for that leadership. At present we have a potential ordinand from a more Anglo catholic tradition and Fran in training. Another woman is at the beginning of the ordination route, with others visiting the Church for a season to experience the worship and leadership that Martin brings. Because of Martin's personal story, he is not judgemental of others, and lets God lead them into new patterns of behaviour, more in line with that expected of Christians. Martin is an extrovert, and enjoys leading worship. He tells us of his beloved Fulham's track record frequently, and has many outside interests.

Able to preach a pretty academic sermon if required, Martin left school at 16 and worked as a photographer, learning about the demands of a people intensive job, where you have to fit into the mores of the people who you are working for. He learnt the 'chameleon trade' early and is now comfortable with all sorts of people. His father (who died when Martin was 16) was an undertaker, so he knows about extreme experiences and how they affect people. He, with Fran, led a youth congregation before ordination, setting up a '*Soul* Survivor' congregation locally prior to ordination and leading another such congregation while a curate. Martin has a deep belief in his vocation to be himself as a priest, and of his calling to this particular place. He is secure in who he is, knowing that he is on a journey and recognizing God's leading for him and his family. Ordained at the (then-average age) of 34, he has the wisdom of years behind him, and time to grow further in ministry.

Martin is frustrated by feeling slightly on the 'edge' of the diocese; having been involved in many aspects of his diocese while a curate, he is now largely outside of the diocesan committees etc., where he could prove a visionary if sometimes challenging voice. He reads a book a month and attends at least one conference annually to ensure he stays up to date, and personally and spiritually nourished. Martin is committed to his church, but knows that he may eventually be called to move on. He would possible fit into a bigger version of the New Wine type of church, but he is a humble man, who would go where he is led by God. Fran is there to provide support and great love for him – he has a bright future in the Church.

How the Church national integrates different wings of the church is a big question – and one at which we're not very successful at the moment. If voices such as Martin are to be heard on the wider stage, the Church must get past its present tendency to label people according to churchmanships and theology, to listen to the ideas and creativity that the different churches bring.

The recipe for a fulfilled life as a vicar? That will vary according to who you are, but the experience of the two wives as 'vicarage' people before they married their present priests undoubtedly helps. Combine that with good boundaries, clear vision and self-worth, and the minister has more chance of staying within the Church, fulfilled and enabling others to find their way too. Two out of the three are also extrovert, (the third has never been through Myers–Briggs) but all three know that they need to be supported in their ministry, and have built systems into their working lives to provide that support and encouragement that we all need. Two of the three are also in their first incumbencies, and haven't been in ministry yet for the 'repeat the same again' syndrome to hit. It will be interesting to watch their progress, and see if after 30 years of ministry (as Peter has) they are still enjoying ministry as much as they clearly are now.

In conclusion

The reasons that different people gave for leaving varied, but none had lost their faith. Many talked of feeling constrained, of having no outlet for their creativity, of a frustration that the role of parish priest meant that they felt as if they could no longer be themselves.

The people who have left ministry now move within the Church, at a greater distance from the centre. One of the benefits of researching this book is that I and those whom I have met intend to set up a support group. Apart from that, and the officiating at various services, most of these ministers now have little 'official' input into a Church that desperately needs their creativity and abilities but finds it hard to work out how to effectively use such a support group if they are not ministering within a recognised area of the Church.

The other strong theme was that the Church had changed during their time in ministry, to the extent that the ministers felt out of step with the majority of 'the Church' as they perceived the institution. Many of them, but not all, are more Catholic than Evangelical and see the perceived rise in power of the evangelical wing of the Church to be excluding rather than including. This is underlined by the ongoing debate about women bishops and gay priests. It could be that moving dioceses would solve that perception, but as everyone who left had a catalogue of reasons, changing one bishop for another is not the answer. It was often that a door had opened, and the person realized that if they didn't walk through it now, they never would – that the opportunity may not present itself once more.

Leaping the vicarage wall is not easy. But, speaking personally, being outside the vicarage is a far more comfortable place to be me.

CHAPTER 8
Where do we go from here?

Writing this book has been the traditional roller coaster that authors often speak of; the ups were catching up with people, some of whom I hadn't seen for many years, the downs were hearing their stories, and then reading similar comments in books that were written at the beginning of the present decade, whose suggestions were applauded and then, seemingly, largely ignored.

I was in parish ministry for 16 years, and my experience limited. But, from that position, and with the wisdom of those who have shared their journeys so generously, I'd like to offer the following suggestions for improving the lot of parish clergy, and so maintaining their ministry.

Expectations

As one of my consulting clergy commented, with clergy terms of service,[1] life should get better for clergy, because they will have a more accurate picture of what a parish expects from them. However, one expectation will be assumed: 'Clergy are still expected, vicariously, to be good, to be good on behalf of others'.[2]

Being good is part of the stress. The recent sit-com *Rev* showed a vicar being – should I say – 'bad'?, certainly 'letting the side down'. Getting drunk, smoking and swearing. Hardly arrestable offenses, but offensive to many readers of the *Church Times*, and I must confess, shocking to myself see on the screen. (Although I cheered too!).

The fact that the local paper has a field day every time a member of the clergy gets a speeding fine, let alone runs off with the organist, shows how far we have to travel in this area. But clergy are human beings – let's take them off the pedestal, for we all have feet of clay:

> Many ministers feel that they need to be perfect. Congregations generally expect that they should! ... Perhaps the greatest source of clergy stress comes from this sense of having to live with a mask, a 'pulpit persona'. The gradual erosion of the freedom to be one's authentic, true self, in favour of a religious performance, undermines the very springs of spiritual and psychological well-being. No wonder church leaders can become difficult people.[3]

The beginning of thorough appraisals/MDR, with the affirmation and accountability that they bring, will also aid clergy expectations of themselves, to be realistic:

> There is fundamentally a two way bargain: clergy desperately need more *affirmation* – support for them as people, valuing the work they do, and protection from the exploitation of their goodwill. The other side of the bargain is the need to be open to much greater *accountability* – good use of their working time, objective scrutiny of their competence, and responsibility for their own personal development. It is important that these two aspects are taken forward hand in hand – accountability without affirmation, resources and training is cruel: affirmation without accountability is an impossible dream.[4]

However, dioceses have to realistic in what they expect clergy to manage:

> At the moment, clergy ... are being stretched ever more thinly in an effort to maintain an untenable status quo.[5]

In August, I went to a local village church for evensong, 1662 style. It was taken, very well, by a reader (lay minister). The vicar was on holiday, but there was also no need for the vicar to take the service. The ten of us made a joyful noise to the Lord, and went home. Excellent. It clearly met a need, and the happy and welcoming (and not very young) congregation had realistic expectations of who would lead the worship. This is rare. Using ordained clergy to undertake tasks that others cannot will need to become a priority in the near future, and folk will need to be helped to have realistic expectations of their clergy.

And the third group who need to be realistic is the people who live in the parish, and especially those who worship regularly.

> The call process in most denominations is flawed in that it makes negotiating a good match difficult for pastors and congregations. One major problem is insufficient honesty and candour in what is essentially a bargaining process in which each party displays its best side and hides its worst. Indeed ... congregations often did not even know what their goals were or did not have the necessary commitment to reach those goals.[6]

Helping congregations to be honest with what they want and what they need will be an enormous boon to clergy who are moving parish, in finding the right place for them. Being honest in recognizing the story of their parish is also critical – show the would-be vicar the skeletons in the closet before their induction, please! How much work they expect from their new vicar is part of the next area of suggestions and hopes.

The working week

> Move to a system of contractual employment for all clergy.[7]

Having a contract, drawn up by the PCC in consultation with a diocesan expert who has helped them through the process, would be of great help to clergy. Clergy who move into posts on common tenure, will receive such a document. This will act both ways – it will tell the minister what the parish want and expect, but it will also defend the minister if the parish suddenly start including another agenda.

> The gap between what ministers would like to do and what they are actually required to do is a problem for seminary educators and denominational officials.[8]

Theological colleges are addressed in a different place.

The problem for many clergy is the pile of 'stuff' which prevents them from ministering.[9] Written 8 years ago, the following quote is still laughable for most clergy, who find switching off almost impossible:

> Consider 50 hours per week to be a reasonable upper limit, and 38 hours per week, a reasonable lower limit, for clergy working hours.[10]

Having a staff team who can pick up much of the admin is hugely advantageous to ministers. Clearly, some areas will be able to provide such people more than others. Perhaps this is a case for the chapter/deanery to share people in a pooling type activity? I once asked someone from a different parish to be my treasurer, as I didn't have anyone who could do that, and her church had more than one such person. It worked very well, and because she came from outside the parish, she sometimes made very helpful observations about the way we had slipped into undesirable habits. Sharing good administrators, secretaries and money people who could perhaps be paid from a shared pot may be a good way to help parishes that are struggling.[11] Freeing up the minister to minister could release time and an enormous burden from clergy who have people skills but find administration a chore.

With my last PCC, we drew up a series of aims and objectives for the parish, as part of our Mission Statement. Now I'm not a great one for jargon, but that's what we called it. They hadn't done this before in that parish. We set out our aims for the next 5 years, and then broke them down.[12] Thus I knew, and they knew, where we were hoping to be in 5 years, but more important for me (as I'm not good at long-term planning) I knew where we wanted to be by the end of the year. So, at the APCM, we could talk about what we'd managed to do, and what we hadn't, and work out strategies as we went along to help achieve more each year. This gave me clear focus, and helped the PCC to realize their part in that. Every year we reviewed, and added and amended. Thus we could see the church moving on, and bask in our little successes. It worked for me.

Clergy need to acknowledge the need for time off in the day, as well as a day off, and take it. Get a dog and walk it, go out on a bike, go for a jog, but do something that gets you out of the house, away from the phone (no mobiles!) and is physical. And the parishioners need to stop sniping if they see you doing such a thing:

> Congregations must learn not to have unreasonable expectations of their clergy.[13]

Time out is critical if clergy are to be fresh and clear thinking – and as most work most evenings, time off during the day is needed to give that space. And physical? Because few clergy are fit, due to sitting in front of computers or steering wheels much of the time. Physical fitness impacts upon mental heath quickly. A fit vicar is a less likely to be depressed vicar. Take at least a day and half off per week. That may mean using a different day as the 'off' one from time to time, but it can be done.

My 'flourishing' archdeacon recognized that his marriage was good because his wife took a day off midweek to be with him. Likewise a respected colleague, still in ministry and just moving to a new parish. Not all clergy can do this, but for those who can – do!

I used to take off Saturday morning if I had a wedding, and as much of Saturday as I could to be with my husband and kids. As well as Friday, not instead of. This means planning your week, as far as possible and prioritizing work.[14] I am a J on Myers–Briggs, so this wasn't too challenging – for those clergy who are P, it's time to work in your shadow for a moment. All clergy carry diaries, and sometimes compete for who has the biggest and busiest, but if you start by taking out an evening and a day and a half, you're well on the way. And don't forget to block out holidays, and book cover well before you go away.

Management training

Savage and Boyd-Macmillan observe:

> Many in church leadership would benefit from management training applied to the context of faith communities ....[15]

Time planning would be part of this, but some sort of MBA type input, with a chance to practise managing a church and chairing meetings could be enormously valuable. Some dioceses are already there, with updated CME and post-ordination training. Hopefully, all will provide this. At present, the already-squeezed colleges and courses do not have the timetable space to commit to this on top of all their other fields of expertise, although some do include managing change as a short course. Ideally, this would be included when ministers have some real experiences to base their learning and reflection upon, such as the MA that I took after several years in the parish.

Boundaries

The parish office and the vicarage

All clergy housing has to include space to be used as a study. Many vicarages also house all sorts of office equipment, as part of the house's legacy, because the parish has nowhere else to store them.

What is the study for? Is it the minister's private study or an office that is for the whole parish? This is for the vicar and PCC to decide, but I would like to suggest that every incumbent has access to an alternative space that is for 'office' work. If the parish has an administrator or secretary, even if they are only very part time, this is where they work. This is where the parish phone rings, rather than the vicarage, this is where wedding couples are seen, rather than the vicarage, and so on. Thus the vicarage could become a family home, not part of the parish property that people walk into without invitation, and so the dog doesn't spend ages barking at all the strangers who arrive on the doorstep. Most important, this is part of the boundary discipline:

> Keeping appropriate boundaries communicates respect towards other people and oneself.[16]

Introducing some sense of privacy would enable clergy families to be families, with some privacy and a life that not everyone is aware of.

Whether the vicarage remains next to the church is also a big factor. People in need will always find the vicarage, but space between where the vicar lives and the church removes the problem of people using the vicarage parking area as an extension to the station car park. Or where everyone 'has always parked' for the mid week service, let alone the wedding congregations. Do I sound a touch hysterical here? This factor has been the straw that broke many a vicar's back. It also means the vicar won't be asked for keys for various events, and other odd duties 'because you're there'.

Clearly defined space and territory is deeply instinctive, and many ministers live with space invaders. Using the vicarage for garden parties and events must be by consultation, not prefaced with 'all the previous vicars were okay with ...' And it would be helpful if the boundary of the vicarage was marked, rather than just merging with the church yard.

The parish phone line may be switchable to the vicarage for emergencies. All clergy now need a parish mobile, and I recommend keeping their own personal number just that – for friends and family. What you do about e-mail needs to be carefully worked out.

Time off, a day out, needs to be just that, and living away from the church would enable time out without interruption. It would also facilitate working too, as the minister is more likely to be left alone.

Coping with the job

As previously suggested, clergy need to be tough:

> Include strategies for developing hardiness and resilience from early stages of clergy training.[17]

Regular supervision input for coping with stress and conflicting demands would be very beneficial for clergy. Likewise a good self-knowledge, including Myers–Briggs factors and Spiritual Styles. This needs repeating every few years, as these can change over time:

> We need to teach more about change in institutions and give folks skill and practice in doing it.[18]

Much of the stress comes from helping people in church to move through periods of change and transition. While clergy are familiar with experiencing both of these states, they are not so practised at facilitating others through it in a constructive, win–win way. CME in these fields would be helpful.

> Ministers are experiencing a lack of support and support systems, especially when they are coping with conflicts.[19]

Many professionals working in similar fields such as social work have ongoing supervision built into their diaries. I remember being told to find a supervisor before I left college – but only in St Albans diocese did I have one. If this could be introduced as a 'must' for all clergy, the benefits would be enormous.

It would also be hugely advantageous if ministers could see that asking for help, and further training, is not a bad thing. Many are almost neurotic about admitting difficulty, or asking for help and advice. A small, well-facilitated group, meeting regularly (maybe like a cell group) could look at the problems that conflict causes clergy without anyone being judged lacking. This group could devise ways of dealing with the conflict, as well as anticipating it and sometimes heading it off. A pilot project in Canterbury diocese has been very successful in helping clergy to work in this way.

Realistic expectations from the Church hierarchy

> More and more of the pastors are saying 'I can't go to that church because of my spouse's job' ... it has affected morale ... making appointments is much harder than it was ten years ago.[20]

The way that we live has changed over the years. We can all look back and say 'it wasn't like that in my day', but what do we gain?

There is a need for ordination selectors to be honest with folk as they are selected about where they may need to be deployed, and recognize that sometimes that sacrifice is too much. Partnerships are equal today, and many partners won't just leave their work to follow an ordained partner to the other end of the diocese, let alone the country. We recognize that moving around affects children and spouses, and we need to work carefully with families to support them and cherish them. After all, they are the front line for cherishing for the clergy.

This may mean that the selection of clergy becomes more targeted, recognizing the need, say, for more people prepared for rural ministry, with large benefices as opposed to somewhere with just one church, near to a large city where the partner can work. We need to see that the Church is becoming more localized as ordination age rises and fewer people can easily relocate, and change our expectations accordingly.

But we also need to help ordinands in training to see that they may not be offered their dream post, and that their vocation may be taking them to somewhere that they may find outside of their comfort zone.

We also need to train clergy in modern communication skills, and keep this ongoing as technology races forward. Thus we can provide imaginative, modern worship that will appeal to the younger members of the population, while recognizing that older people will not find this attractive.

Where does ministry take place?

When I was exploring what to do after the parish, some people clearly thought that I had lost my sense of vocation. A wise friend exclaimed 'but it's like moving from general practice to being a consultant' and that's exactly how I see it, but I usually have to explain. Moving out of a parish frees me to undertake what is a very specialist ministry. There are a few people out there with the same skills, but only a few are ordained. Bringing my knowledge of theology and overview of spirituality makes what I bring unique. And I couldn't achieve that when I was in the parish – I didn't have the time.

Felix and George would echo what I believe. The women and men who are ministering in creative and imaginative ways are exploring ways of being true to their vocation, but it's not in the parish ministry mould:

> Often, creative people will feel constrained by the proce-
> dures and rules of a bureaucracy. Such people will move
> to the margins or away from formal church involvement,
> while still affirming the gospel.[21]

As the Church loses more and more diocesan specialists, I believe there will be a need for more people like myself – the secular world is jammed with consultants who operate in exactly the same way. Usually older, with workplace achievements to draw upon, alongside experience and specialist knowledge, consultants enable many of the larger organizations to flourish. The Church is learning how to work with people like myself and recognize the contribution that we make. Felix description of himself as a 'loose canon' reflects very much how I feel about my relationship with the church:

How can the Church recognize and support those who need to exercise their ministry in a more creative way, those who think 'outside the box', people such as myself and others? Perhaps we can all go down the permission to officiate route,[22] but then there is a clear pecking order between stipendiary priests and the others. A clear example of this is that the 'others' often receive important mailings a day or two after stipendiary priests in my experience. We need to let go of pecking orders, and all be equal, and see that reflected in how the 'hierarchy' deal with their clergy.

The critical thing for me in all the conversations that I had is that none of the ministers had lost their faith. They all just felt called to exercise it in a slightly different way to the traditional vision that the Church has for her clergy. And we recognize that what we do now draws profoundly on our vocation to be priests; 'it's ministry Jim, but not as we know it'. We also use our skills gained through years in the parish, and understand the limitations with people that we train and work alongside. My present work draws together my teaching and ministry skills in a wonderful way – two vocations in one lifestyle.

Many of us have 'liberal' views, and find the way that the church is moving, towards a more hard-line evangelical stance, uncomfortable. But we moved out because we felt called to exercise a ministry that the parish was stifling. Not because it intended to, or in any conscious way, but because there was too little time and energy left at the end of each day to be able to use the gifts that we feel are God given. When people ask me about what I do now, I point out that it uses all the gifts and experience from teaching, from parish ministry and my study, to be able to serve the Church in a very special way. This is the next part of my journey of faith; I have no doubt about it. But, as someone who still loves the C of E very deeply most of the time, I would love to be part of a recognized form of ministry, along with my colleagues who are out there working alongside the Church.

For people who exercise their creativity, the parish can be constraining and ultimately life draining. The joy of researching this book is that none of us have lost our faith: we still have our vocations, but they have moved out from the constraints of the Church and are now being used to work with people to explore their faith more creatively and within a far wider context. To leap the vicarage wall requires nerve, vision and support, allied with the realization that vocation and ministry still exist 'out there', in the wider world where me and my colleagues who've made the leap, are still working for the Kingdom of God.

APPENDIX I

Common tenure on two sides of A4

A new form of tenure for clergy office holders called common tenure is due to take effect from 31 January 2011. Clergy and other office holders will continue to be appointed as vicars, rectors, assistant curates, priests in charge and so on. Under these new arrangements, a post may only be limited to a fixed term in certain specified circumstances[1] and the great majority of office holders may remain in a particular post until they resign or retire.

Common tenure will confer in addition the following *rights*:

- an entitlement to be provided with a written statement of particulars setting out the terms of their appointment
- an entitlement to an uninterrupted rest period of not less than 24 hours in any period of seven days
- an entitlement to 36 days' annual leave
- an entitlement to maternity, paternity, parental and adoption leave in accordance with directions given by the Archbishops' Council as Central Stipends Authority
- an entitlement to request time off, or adjustments to the duties of the office, to care for dependants in accordance with directions given by the Archbishops' Council as Central Stipends Authority
- an entitlement to spend time on certain public duties other than the duties of the office, with the matter being determined by the bishop if there is any dispute
- access to a grievance procedure

- a right of appeal to an employment tribunal if removed from office on grounds of capability.

Incumbents will continue to have formal legal ownership of the parsonage house by virtue of holding the benefice as corporation sole, and their property rights will be unaffected. Other office holders will acquire the following rights:

- the right to accommodation 'reasonably suitable for the purpose'
- the right to object to the disposal, improvement, demolition or reduction of their house of residence
- the right to have the house of residence kept in good repair by a relevant housing provider (in most cases this will be the diocesan parsonages board)
- access to arbitration where there is a dispute about the performance of the respective obligations of the housing provider and the office holder which cannot be resolved by the grievance procedure
- where they are not already entitled to compensation, an entitlement to receive to up one year's compensation if displaced as a result of pastoral reorganization.

Common tenure will confer the following *obligations*:

- to participate and co-operate in ministerial development review (MDR)
- to participate in arrangements approved by the diocesan bishop for continuing ministerial education (CME)
- to inform a person nominated by the bishop when unable to perform the duties of office through sickness
- to undergo a medical examination where the bishop has reasonable grounds for concern about the office holder's physical or mental health.

The legislation introduces a capability procedure which may be instigated where an office holder's performance gives cause for concern, and which may, in the last resort, lead to removal from office in cases where performance is not satisfactory and fails to improve. The law affecting patronage and the appointments procedure remains unchanged. The Clergy Discipline Measure 2003 and the Canons continue to apply to all clergy whether on common tenure or not.

The Terms of Service legislation will require diocesan bishops:

- to make and keep under review a MDR scheme containing arrangements for a person nominated by the bishop to conduct a review with each office holder in the diocese at least once every two years
- to have regard to guidance issued by the Archbishops' Council when carrying out MDR
- to ensure that a written record of the outcome of MDR is kept and to have it signed by the office holder and the reviewer
- to use reasonable endeavours to ensure that office holders in the diocese are afforded opportunities to participate in CME that is appropriate for their ministerial development
- to make appropriate arrangements to ensure that office holders in training posts are provided with suitable training and are afforded time off work as is necessary to complete it
- to nominate an officer of the diocese with responsibility for providing statements of particulars and receiving reports of sickness absence
- to have regard to the Archbishops' Council's codes of practice concerning the capability and grievance procedures.

All new appointments after 31 January 2011 will be on common tenure.

The following will transfer automatically onto common tenure on 31 January 2011: assistant curates, priests in charge, team vicars, residentiary canons on fixed term appointments.

The diocesan bishop is required to write to all clergy with the freehold (including incumbents, team rectors, deans, archdeacons, and residentiary canons not on fixed term appointments) as soon as practicable after 31 January 2011 to ask if they wish to transfer onto common tenure. These clergy remain on their existing terms, unless and until they agree to move onto common tenure (which they may do at any time) or leave their current post.

Source: http://www.cofe.anglican.org/lifeevents/ministry/workof mindiv/dracsc/rctshomepage/commsresources/2sides.pdf (June 2010).

APPENDIX 2

Summary of diocesan licensed ministers 2008

Ref. no.	Diocese	Province	Full-time stipendiary clergy			Part-time stipendiary clergy			Non-stipendiary clergy			Ordained local ministers			Total clergy (stipendiary, NSM and OLM)	Total readers and Church Army	Total clergy, readers and Church Army
			Men	Women	Total	Men	Women	Total	Men	Women	Total	Men	Women	Total	Total	Total	Total
1	Bath & Wells	C	168	40	208	11	5	16	36	30	66	0	0	0	290	280	570
2	Birmingham	C	123	45	168	3	4	7	20	23	43	0	0	0	218	178	396
3	Blackburn	Y	159	17	176	3	3	6	27	25	52	0	0	0	234	166	400
4	Bradford	Y	85	14	99	6	7	13	20	24	44	0	0	0	156	103	259
5	Bristol	C	103	29	132	1	4	5	22	23	45	0	0	0	191	175	366
6	Canterbury	C	113	24	137	3	3	6	26	31	57	5	4	9	228	117	345
7	Carlisle	Y	120	25	145	2	3	5	23	23	46	13	15	28	200	105	305
8	Chelmsford	C	315	72	387	5	5	10	49	52	101	2	2	4	499	373	872
9	Chester	Y	197	46	243	9	8	17	31	36	67	1	0	1	327	370	697
10	Chichester	C	273	19	292	5	2	7	57	32	89	0	0	0	388	182	570
11	Coventry	C	98	18	116	4	3	7	12	22	34	0	0	0	165	161	326
12	Derby	Y	130	25	155	0	0	0	22	26	48	3	5	8	203	251	454
13	Durham	C	151	38	189	8	3	11	22	25	47	0	0	0	252	148	400
14	Ely	C	105	37	142	5	4	9	28	29	57	1	4	5	208	147	355
15	Exeter	C	189	34	223	14	8	22	36	27	63	0	0	0	308	206	514
16	Gloucester	C	108	31	139	4	4	8	43	39	82	3	6	9	238	137	375
17	Guildford	C	145	30	175	3	9	12	34	45	79	29	25	54	320	128	448

#	Diocese	Prov.	1	2	3	4	5	6	7	8	9	10	11	12	13	14	15
18	Hereford	C	69	28	97	0	2	2	14	25	39	4	7	11	149	84	233
19	Leicester	C	105	37	142	4	2	6	24	22	46	0	0	0	194	143	337
20	Lichfield	C	243	55	298	4	9	13	25	35	60	32	30	62	433	312	745
21	Lincoln	C	138	35	173	2	1	3	13	22	35	11	12	23	234	164	398
22	Liverpool	Y	162	49	211	0	1	1	15	14	29	12	18	30	271	307	578
23	London	C	447	68	515	7	11	18	122	56	178	0	0	0	711	221	932
24	Manchester	Y	185	56	241	3	3	6	29	20	49	40	40	80	376	156	532
25	Newcastle	Y	106	31	137	1	1	2	13	18	31	10	8	18	188	95	283
26	Norwich	C	158	35	193	2	7	9	21	20	41	22	23	45	288	190	478
27	Oxford	C	286	89	375	6	2	8	104	88	192	19	31	50	625	225	850
28	Peterborough	C	112	29	141	2	2	4	19	19	38	0	0	0	183	137	320
29	Portsmouth	C	94	18	112	0	3	3	17	39	56	0	0	0	171	90	261
30	Ripon & Leeds	Y	94	36	130	3	0	3	22	15	37	0	0	0	170	103	273
31	Rochester	C	185	29	214	4	10	14	24	36	60	0	0	0	288	260	548
32	St Albans	C	187	65	252	2	6	8	47	50	97	0	1	1	358	222	580
33	St Edms & Ipswich	C	114	27	141	3	7	10	22	25	47	18	28	46	244	168	412
34	Salisbury	C	168	44	212	0	0	0	28	33	61	23	31	54	327	109	436
35	Sheffield	Y	120	37	157	0	5	5	15	8	23	0	0	0	185	194	379
36	Sodor & Man	Y	12	1	13	0	0	0	7	1	8	2	0	2	23	28	51
37	Southwark	C	268	76	344	3	5	8	95	107	202	0	0	0	554	182	736
38	Southwell	Y	107	43	150	2	3	5	20	22	42	0	0	0	197	303	500
39	Truro	C	91	18	109	2	0	2	24	20	44	6	4	10	165	83	248
40	Wakefield	Y	113	39	152	1	2	3	19	21	40	9	16	25	220	125	345
41	Winchester	C	190	21	211	4	3	7	42	40	82	0	0	0	300	283	583
42	Worcester	C	113	30	143	0	1	1	9	19	28	0	0	0	172	124	296
43	York	Y	183	43	226	5	4	9	47	36	83	0	1	1	319	250	569
44	Europe	C	118	13	131	0	0	0	25	19	44	0	0	0	175	72	247
	Province of Canterbury		4,956	1,121	6,077	103	122	225	1,060	1,054	2,114	189	222	411	8,827	5,404	14,231
	Province of York		1,794	475	2,269	43	43	86	310	288	598	76	89	165	3,118	2,453	5,571
	Church of England		6,750	1,596	8,346	146	165	311	1,370	1,342	2,712	265	311	576	11,945	7,857	19,802

Please see notes overleaf.

The above figures include only those ministers who were working within the diocesan framework as at 31 December 2008. The Archbishop of Canterbury and ordained members of his staff at Lambeth Palace are classed as extra-diocesan and are not included in these figures. Reader and Church Army figures do not include PTO and emeriti, or ordained Church Army evangelists. C, Province of Canterbury; NSM, non-stipendiary minister; OLM, others from a more Anglo catholic tradition; Y, Province of York.

Source: Information from Research and Statistics, Archbishops' Council, www.cofe.anglian.org/info/statistics.

APPENDIX 3

Full-time stipendiary clergy losses and gains 1990–2008

The following tables are based on the numbers of clergy leaving and entering the clergy payroll (excluding the Diocese in Europe), which is held currently by the Church Commissioners. The losses and gains recorded include people that have moved to and from the Diocese in Europe, to and from posts which are funded by external agencies, such as National Health Service Trusts, the Prison Service, mission agencies or schools, and between stipendiary and self-supporting ministry or full- and part-time.

The total number of full-time stipendiary clergy at the end of 2008 was 8,215 (6,632 men plus 1,583 women). The number of full-time stipendiary clergy plus the whole-time equivalent of part-time stipendiary clergy within the Clergy Apportionment process was 8,369, which is slightly lower than the 8,406 projected at the start of 2008.

Annual losses and gains, full-time stipendiary clergy: men

Year	Deaths in service	Retirements	Other losses	Total losses	Ordinations	Other gains	Total gains	Net loss	No. on 31 December 2008
1990	29	289	204	522	282	190	472	50	10,480
1995	27	338	236	601	245	130	375	226	9,440
1996	29	363	241	633	201	137	338	295	9,145
1997	21	357	207	585	186	129	315	270	8,875
1998	24	329	187	540	174	144	318	222	8,653
1999	25	317	201	543	199	150	349	194	8,459
2000	17	349	182	548	223	151	374	174	8,285
2001	15	359	210	584	186	147	333	251	8,034
2002	18	332	180	530	195	123	318	212	7,822
2003	19	310	184	513	181	123	304	209	7,613
2004	11	285	199	495	143	110	253	242	7,371
2005	17	252	179	448	155	141	296	152	7,219
2006	16	262	165	443	128	97	225	218	7,001
2007	12	274	179	465	161	76	237	228	6,773
2008	8	256	173	437	191	86	277	160	6,613

Annual losses and gains, full-time stipendiary clergy: women

Year	Deaths in service	Retirements	Other losses	Total losses	Ordinations	Other gains	Total gains	Net loss	No. on 31 December 2008
1990	1	11	39	51	79	29	108	57	596
1995	1	19	55	75	65	47	112	37	820
1996	2	17	41	60	67	32	99	39	859
1997	1	19	25	45	57	48	105	60	919
1998	0	16	28	44	67	41	108	64	983
1999	2	16	39	57	78	57	135	78	1,061
2000	2	19	49	70	90	46	136	66	1,127
2001	3	27	52	82	95	51	146	64	1,191
2002	1	35	54	90	106	54	160	70	1,251
2003	2	27	46	75	120	47	167	102	1,353
2004	1	28	71	100	92	51	143	43	1,396
2005	2	40	72	114	99	78	177	63	1,459
2006	2	34	60	96	92	40	132	36	1,495
2007	1	38	57	95	100	32	132	36	1,531
2008	0	38	69	107	116	39	155	48	1,579

Source: Church Commissioners.

APPENDIX 4

St Somewhere mission statement

Living faith in **** Village**
Our common life flows out of our worship of God, Father, Son and Holy Spirit, as expressed within the Church of England.

Aims
Proclaim the Good News of Jesus Christ to all.

Be a worshipping community that encourages all to learn about their faith through regular worship, study and fellowship groups..

Meet regularly at social activities that will appeal to all ages (some events will be for a specific group).

Serve the people of the parish through Occasional Offices, through easy access to the Church, through easy access to the Hall and to the people of the Church.

Encourage the people of the parish to worship with the regular congregation, especially at certain times of the year.

Always be seeking ways in which we can serve the people of the parish.

Continue to encourage links with local schools.

Offer a wide diversity of worship, well led and with scope to grow and change.

Objectives

2007

Increase the number of roles for children to participate in the Liturgy.

Widen our liturgical style.

Critically review our inclusion of children in our worship.

Review admin and communication within the Church.

2008

Ministry team to continue to grow; (suggested) another reader and PA.

Increase congregation (compared to 2000) by 40 per cent.

Lower average age of congregation by 5 years compared to 2004.

More lay leadership across Church activities.

Possible mid-week service at Old Bexley School.

2009

Repair/renovate the organ.

Redecorate remaining areas of church.

Possible re-ordering of Church.

APPENDIX 5

Curate working agreement

DIOCESES of CANTERBURY and ROCHESTER
Sample working agreement between the incumbent and the curate

Praying together
The curate does not live in the parish but some miles away in ***** *****. In view of this she will usually make her own arrangements for her morning prayers and this will be done at her home before making her journey to the parish.

However morning prayer will be said together in church at 9.00 a.m. on Monday morning and both morning and Evening Prayer will be said together in church when practical. For this we shall use Common Worship Daily Prayer with psalms and readings from the Common Worship Lectionary.

There will be regular staff meetings with other members of the ministry team and this will include prayer and worship in which we will both participate and both lead.

Informal prayer with and for each other will be a natural inclusion in our specified times of supervision.

Public worship
With the exception of holidays, retreats and residential study the curate will be present and robed at all the principal public services on Sundays, Festivals, Holy Days and Saints Days as observed in the parish.

With the incumbent she will share the presidency at the Sunday 8.00 a.m. and 9.30 a.m. celebrations of the Eucharist and will share in the Ministry of Healing as arranged

The curate will preside alternate weeks at the 10.30 a.m. said Holy Communion on Wednesdays and the 11.00 a.m. service at the worship centre.

The curate will act as deacon at the Eucharist as per the rota agreed with the other members of the ministry team.

The curate will preach as per the rota agreed with the others members of the ministry team – about once per month at the 9.30 a.m. Eucharist and as agreed at the monthly All-Age Family Service.

As a full member of the ministry team the curate will be prepared to give and receive constructive criticism of sermons delivered.

Staff meetings

The curate will meet with the incumbent and other staff members as appropriate on a weekly basis to discuss and plan diary and ministry activities for the week and to share information – this will normally be on a Monday morning. We will aim to have an 'away-day' or longer residential meeting to plan particular events or initiatives and to develop our ministerial activities.

The curate will meet with the incumbent one to one once every fortnight for a two-hour supervision session to reflect on aspects of her ministerial experience as recorded in her journal.

In addition the curate and the incumbent will meet with the full ministry team once every two months to plan ministry and preaching rotas, to discuss any relevant pastoral matters and to pray and worship together.

The team will support and encourage each other and share and reflect with honesty and openness.

The incumbent will be available at any time outside the agreed schedule for consultation and help.

Professional behaviour

The incumbent and the curate agree that there will be absolute confidentiality between themselves. Further they agree that they will respect the confidentiality of any third party they are ministering to and only share with each other what the third party permits.

In addition the curate agrees to support the incumbent and be loyal to his leadership and role in the parish and the incumbent agrees to be loyal to her as a professional colleague and fellow minister of the gospel.

Work balance and areas of special responsibility

The curate will experience and take part in all aspects of parochial life and activity working with and along side the incumbent in particular but also with other members of the ministry team as occasion and opportunity allow.

Particular areas of responsibility will emerge in discussion with the incumbent and the curate has full authority to work with other members of the ministry team, the churchwardens, the PCC, Sunday School and other leaders in these tasks.

Role in the wider community and Church

The curate will play a full and active role in deanery synod, deanery chapter and the diocese as opportunity arises. She will also work with the incumbent in fostering links with the local schools and other local organizations, again as opportunity presents itself. At this stage it is not possible to predict how much time this may require but there will be full negotiation between the curate and the incumbent.

Communication in the parish

There will be a meeting between the curate and the incumbent at least once every week to discuss diary dates and all ministerial activity, to give and receive news and deal will all matters of mutual concern. There are opportunities to talk at various times and there will also be regular meetings with the other members of the ministry team as arranged.

Time for study

It is recognized by the incumbent and the PCC, and accepted by both, that this is a training appointment and the curate will be encouraged and enabled to fulfil all the requirements of Continuing Ministerial Education, indeed this will be treated as a priority when it comes to fixing diary dates. In connection with this the curate will take at least one day per week as a study day (in addition to her day off).

Time off

It is recognized that finding the right pattern for time off will depend very much on individual circumstances. The guiding principles are as follows:

- in any 12-month period a total of 116 non-working days are allocated
- these are to be negotiated with the incumbent but will include: (i) eight Bank Holidays, (ii) 30 days annual leave (to include five Sundays), and (iii) at least one whole day off per week

It is recognized that flexibility will be needed to accommodate the inevitable peaks and troughs of parish life and the above guiding principle allows for such flexibility.

Expenses and fees

All working expenses will be met; the curate will submit an expenses claim form to the Hon. Treasurer on or about the first Sunday of each month and the claim will be met by cheque. Car expenses will be paid at the recommended diocesan rate. All parochial fees belong to the PCC and the curate will not receive any fees.

Personal and spiritual development

The curate will regard the development of her prayer and spiritual life as a high priority. She will continue to meet with her spiritual director as and when appropriate and will have an annual retreat – this will not be part of her time off but in addition to it.

Diocesan training

The curate and the incumbent are formally committed to the full KCME programme.

Commitment to the wider Church

When the curate is invited to any form of ministry outside the parish she will discuss it with the incumbent before accepting the invitation, in return the incumbent agrees to discuss his own pattern of ministry and diary dates with the curate so that both incumbent and curate are aware of each others commitments.

Ministry review

The incumbent will undertake an annual review in accordance with the checklist as published in the 'Handbook for Training Incumbents' and send a report to the director of KCME.

Revision of this working agreement

This agreement will be reviewed at least annually as part of the above annual review procedure and at other times by mutual agreement. We agree to sign, date and send any such revised agreement to the director of KCME.

APPENDIX 6

Retirement statistics

2007 statistics from the Church of England Pensions board show:

- 15 per cent of retirements were due to disability/ill health
- around one in three of these are due to stress/anxiety/ depression.

These levels were stable over the previous ten years but the proportion retiring for other reasons has increased.

For details of recent retirements, including those who retired early on health grounds, see The Church of England Pensions Board Annual Report 2009 (p. 45), available at http://www.cofe. anglican.org/about/cepb/annualreport/ar2009.pdf.

Source: Information from Research and Statistics, Archbishops' Council, www.cofe.anglian.org/info/statistics.

Notes

Introduction

1 Lewis-Anthony, 2009, p. 215.

Chapter 1

1 The vicar's story features in chapter 7.
2 Lamont, 2004.
3 www.assemblies.org.uk.

Chapter 2

1 Davie, 1994, p. 142.
2 St Francis is quoted as saying 'Spread the gospel, use words when necessary'.
3 Lewis-Anthony, 2009, p. 42, 135.
4 Savage & Boyd-Macmillan, 2007, p. 131.
5 Warren, 2002, p. 28.
6 Savage & Boyd-Macmillan, 2007, p. 131.
7 See Cray, 2006.
8 www.messychurch.org.uk.
9 Bayes *et al.*, 2009, p. 134.
10 Ibid., p. 12.
11 Lewis-Anthony, 2009, p. 50.
12 Bayes *et al.*, 2009, p. 2.
13 www.ctbi.org.uk.

Chapter 3

1 Produced by Big Talk for BBC 2010.
2 Warren, 2002, p. 83, citing Francis, L. J. and Jones, S. H. *Psychological Perspectives on Christian Ministry*.
3 Rowe, 1990.
4 Savage & Boyd-Macmillan, 2007, p. 83.
5 Ibid., 2007, p. 57.
6 Hoge & Wenger, 2005, pp. 93-95.

7 http://www.enneagraminstitute.com/ (September 2010).

8 Watts *et al.*, 2002, p. 47.

9 Bellous & Csinos, 2009.

10 From the introduction to the assessment booklet, 'Spiritual styles, assessing what really matters', Bellous, J. E., Csinos, D. M. and Peltomaki, D. A. (2009), Canada: Tall Pines Press.

Chapter 4

1 A provincial episcopal visitor (popularly known as a flying bishop) in the Church of England is a bishop assigned to minister to clergy and parishes who do not in conscience accept the ministry of women priests.

2 Training for the Ordained local ministry ceased in September 2010.

3 Savage & Boyd-Macmillan, 2007, p. 133.

4 Burton & Burton, 2009, p. 47 ff.

5 Griffiths, 2009, p. 294.

6 Lewis & Lewis, 1983, p. 10.

7 Griffiths, 2009.

8 MA in Pastoral Theology, part time through the Cambridge Theological Federation, accredited by Anglia Ruskin University.

9 Burton & Burton, 2009, p.84.

10 Hay & Nye, 2006.

11 Using 'jargon' to mean a system of language that is familiar to those who use it regularly, but not to newcomers. The word 'sin' is typical – not on the mouths of many people outside of religious circles, but we expect newcomers to understand this very sophisticated concept, and the tiny word that we use to sum it up without any real explanation when they come to church. The typical reading age for Anglican liturgy is about 10–12; *The Times* rather than the *Sun*. And we all know which of those two titles has the bigger circulation, and not just for page 3 reasons.

12 Burton & Burton, 2009, p.102.

13 Ibid., 2009, p. 78.

14 Warren, 2007.

15 Savage & Boyd-Macmillan, 2007, p. 88.

Chapter 5

1 Warren, 2002, p.80.

2 Wright, 2009, p.39.

3 Ibid., p.2.

4 Via the Cambridge Federation of Theological Colleges/Anglia Ruskin University.

5 Wright, 2009, p.59.

6 Hoge & Wenger, 2005, p. 47.

7 See chapter 7.

8 Hoge & Wenger, 2005, p.76.

9 Savage & Boyd-Macmillan, 2007, p. 149.

10 Hoge & Wenger, 2005, p. 93.

11 Ibid., p. 95.

12 *Guardian*. 'Author leaves religion against homosexuality, birth control and science'. 31 July 2010.

Chapter 6

1 *Church of England Newspaper* has a more evangelical slant, hence a slightly different set of positions are advertised.

2 Society of Martha and Mary, 2002, p. 13.

3 Church of England official figures are rounded out to the nearest 10.

4 Society of Martha and Mary, 2002, p. 25.

5 Burton & Burton, 2009, p. 190.

6 Society of Martha and Mary, 2002, p. 21.

7 Hoge & Wenger, 2005, p. 167.

8 Savage & Boyd-Macmillan, 2007, p. 135.

9 In 2000, one parish described itself as having the branch of Tesco that sold the most champagne in the country!

10 Savage & Boyd-Macmillan, 2007, p. 133.

11 Hoge & Wenger, 2005, p. 150.

12 Warren, 2002, p. 69.

13 Ibid., p. 56.

14 Wright, 2009, p. 145.

15 Wright, 2009, p. 7, citing Furlong, 2000.

Chapter 7

1 Warren, 2002, p. 76.

2 Ibid., p. 101.

3 Wright, 2009, p. 145.

4 Lewis-Anthony, 2009, p. 215.

5 From Revd. Mark Bailey, *Church Times*, Letters 30 July 2010.

6 *Church Times*, 23 April 2010.

7 Lewis-Anthony, 2009, p. 62, citing Savage, S. (2006), 'On the analyst's couch: psychological perspectives on congregations and clergy' in *The Future of the Parish System: shaping the Church of England for the 21st century*, ed. Stephen Croft (London: Church House Publishing) 2006

8 Wright, 2009, p. 7, citing Furlong, 2000.

9 *Church Times* 16 April 2010.

10 Burton, p. 23.

11 See Appendix 6 for recent statistics.

12 A table listing how many people leave parish ministry is found in Appendix 3. The number leaving annually, apart from deaths and retirement, is between 3 and 4 per cent of the stipendiary work force.

13 Warren, 2002, p. 95.

14 I am grateful to Rosemary Lain-Priestley, who introduced me to several such women, who are working creatively to fulfil their vocations both priests and mothers.

15 Hoge & Wenger, 2005, p. 45.

16 Ibid., p. 144.

17 Daisy's comment is common among 'clergy couples' although the Church warns of the difficulty of giving both people in a couple stipendiary posts due to the problems of location and not being able to live in two vicarages. Some dioceses are more imaginative than others..

18 Hoge & Wenger, 2005, p. 66.

19 Warren, 2002.

20 Davie, 1994, p. 108.

21 Lewis-Anthony, 2009, p. 164.

22 See http://www.cofe.anglican.org/about/churchlawlegis/clergydiscipline/.

Chapter 8

1 See Appendix 1.

2 Lewis-Anthony, 2009, p. 41.

3 Savage & Boyd-Macmillan, 2007, p. 135.

4 Society of Martha and Mary, 2002 (from 'A brief overview').

5 Ibid., p. 11.

6 Hoge & Wenger, 2005, p. 212.

7 Society of Martha and Mary, 2002, p. 51.

8 Hoge & Wenger, 2005, p. 119.

9 *Church Times* of 16 April 2010 featured an advertisement for a house for duty, minus admin post. It is still vacant at the time of writing.

10 Society of Martha and Mary, 2002, p. 53.

11 Erith deanery in Rochester diocese shares a deanery youth worker.

12 See Appendix 4.

13 Warren, 2002, p. 209.

14 Lamont & Lamont, 2001.

15 Savage & Boyd-Macmillan, 2007, p. 137.

16 Ibid., p. 148.

17 Society of Martha and Mary, 2002, p. 29.

18 Hoge & Wenger, 2005, p. 159.

19 Ibid., p. 198.

20 Ibid., p. 155.

21 Savage & Boyd-Macmillan, 2007 p. 118.

22 Permission to officiate: a licence to minister in a particular diocese, which means you are included in the dissemination of information and aware of training opportunities etc.

Appendix

1 The main categories are as follows: posts designated as created to cover another office holder's absence from work; posts held by office holders over 70; posts designated as training posts, posts designated as subject to sponsorship funding; posts designated as probationary office; posts created by bishop's mission order under the Dioceses, Pastoral and Mission Measure or held by an office holder over 70; or posts held in conjunction with another office or employment, which come to an end at the same time as the office or employment with which they are held in conjunction. In addition, Regulation 30 provides that, where the mission and pastoral committee of the diocese has invited the views of interested parties on proposals for pastoral reorganization, it will be possible, as an alternative to suspending presentation, to appoint an incumbent subject to pastoral reorganization, in which case the post comes to an end if the pastoral scheme is made within 5 years, or becomes permanent if the scheme is not made.

Bibliography

Bayes, P. and Sledge, T. with Holbrook, J., Rylands, M. and Seeley, M. (2009), *Mission Shaped Parish*. London: Church House Publishing.

Bellous, J. E. and Csinos, D. M. (2009), 'Spiritual styles: creating an environment to nurture spiritual wholeness', *International Journal of Children's Spirituality*, 14(3), 213–24.

Burton, J. and Burton, C. (2009), *Public People, Private Lives*. London: Continuum.

Cray, G. (2006), *Mission Shaped Church*. London: Church House Publishing.

Davie, G. (1994), *Religion in Britain Since 1945*. Oxford: Blackwell.

Furlong, M. (2000), *C of E – The State It's In*. London: Hodder and Stoughton.

Griffiths, M. (2009), *One Generation From Extinction*. Oxford: Monarch Publishing.

Hay, D and Nye, R. (2006), *The Spirit of the Child*. London: Jessica Kingsley Publishing.

Hoge, D. R. and Wenger, J. E. (2005), *Pastors In Transition: why clergy leave local church ministry*. Grand Rapids, Michigan: Eerdmans.

Lamont, R. (2004), 'A comparison of the effect of storytelling on the spirituality of children aged 9 and 10', (unpublished MA (Pastoral Theology) dissertation, Anglia Polytechnic University [now Anglia Ruskin University]).

Lamont, R. (2007), *Understanding Children, Understanding God*. London: SPCK Publishing.

Lamont, R. and Lamont, G. (2001), *Work Life Balance.* London: Sheldon Press.

Lewis, R and Lewis, G. (1983), *Inductive Preaching: helping people listen.* Illinois: Crossways Books.

Lewis-Anthony, J. (2009), *If You Meet George Herbert On The Road, Kill Him.* London: Continuum.

Percy, M. (2006), *Clergy: the origin of the species.* London: Continuum.

Rowe, D. (1990), *Beyond Fear.* London: Fontana

Savage, S. and Boyd-Macmillan, E. (2007), *The Human Face of the Church.* Norwich: Canterbury Press.

Society of Martha and Mary, The (2002), 'Affirmation and accountability'. Exeter: The Society of Martha and Mary

Warren, Y (2002), *The Cracked Pot: the state of today's Anglican clergy.* Stowmarket: Kevin Mayhew.

Watts, F., Nye, R. and Savage, S. (2002), *Psychology for Christian Ministry.* London: Routledge.

Wright, P. (2009), 'The function of ministerial development review in the Church of England'. (unpublished DMin thesis, University of Wales).

Printed in Great Britain
by Amazon.co.uk, Ltd.,
Marston Gate.